the same sex

the
same
sex

an appraisal of homosexuality

Ralph W. Weltge, editor

Wardell B. Pomeroy / William Simon / John H. Gagnon
Evelyn Hooker / Roger L. Shinn / Neale A. Secor
Gilbert M. Cantor / Lewis I. Maddocks / Foster Gunnison, Jr.
Franklin E. Kameny / Barbara B. Gittings

pilgrim press
philadelphia / boston

Contents

the homophile movement

Introduction

This book is about homosexuality, which means literally "the same sex." In its generic sense the word homosexual includes numerous activities and social transactions between persons of the same gender. The all-male board of directors, the businessman's club, the army, the girl's school, the religious order, and churchwomen's circles are all "homosexual" in this primary sense of the word. For all are sexually segregated forms of human association and endeavor.

Each of these groups would also react against inclusion in such a category, indicating how usage of the word is normally confined to a referent of sexual activity per se, and that it connotes negatively sanctioned behavior at that. In the popular mind, public law, and the human disciplines, homosexuality means some degree or form of sexual activity between persons of the same sex.

Few other issues, by simply being mentioned, can arouse more fears, myths, questions, and prompt negative reactions. Homosexuality is often met with humor in order to mask its threat. Perhaps it is axiomatic that people fear most and understand least those human phenomena in which they have little experience and no reliable knowledge to aid comprehension.

The issue of homosexuality is usually discussed in just such an atmosphere of ignorance where highly subjective judgments and personal feelings are the only sources of authority. And often lurking beneath the discussion is a substratum of individual fantasies and collective anxieties which impede rational inquiry. More is known about homosexuality than this cultural fund of opinion and prejudice. One purpose of this book is to make that knowledge more available.

The generation that lives after both Freud and Kinsey is able to talk more easily and publicly about sex. In fact, the media are saturated with sex, as if it were a recent discovery. What has been discovered by everyone is that sex has gone public in terms of language, icons, and the published data of sex research. Old inhibitions and taboos have fallen, releasing a plethora of talk about sex. The public discussion it has produced would have been unthinkable even a generation ago.

Moving the discussion of sex from the private sphere into the public arena has posed the issue of homosexuality with such frankness that it can no longer be ignored by the church and other institutions. Homosexuality is now a public issue which warrants discussion and reappraisal by the very social and political structures which define and defend the laws and mores of society. This is particularly appropriate given the emergence of sex research which begins to furnish, for the first time in any generation, reliable behavioral data on which to rethink the issue, form opinion, and frame the laws.

This volume is intended to serve as a resource for individual or group study and discussion of the issue of homosexuality. The symposium format was purposely chosen because it allows diverse points of view to be presented, in terms of both interdisciplinary representation and divergent perspectives within a single discipline. The book is a conversation—and sometimes an argument—between sex researchers, ethicists, lawyers, and homosexuals themselves. All need to be heard from if one is going to be intelligent as well as fair in exploring this issue.

Each author writes in his own integrity and from his particular competence in dealing with this issue. The contributors represent some of the most thoughtful and best-qualified persons that can be obtained in the particular fields chosen for representation. And in each case the author's credentials are given in a footnote on the first page of his chapter.

Hopefully this book will contribute to the emerging dialogue between the churches and the homophile community. Being no more than five years old this conversation is still a rather uneasy and tentative rapprochement. The mind of the churches remains almost closed on this issue, and the level of trust in the homophile community is still low with respect to the church. But talks have begun largely through the efforts of men working in single young adult ministries in urban areas. Attempting new forms of ministry with the new generation has resulted in church access to various generational subcultures alien to the traditional styles of church life.

The impetus for this book came from a United Church of Christ staff consultation on homosexuality, and six of the authors were present at that meeting. The Division of Christian Education, United Church Board for Homeland Ministries, sponsored the consultation and found a concert of interest in the issue with the Council for Christian Social Action of the UCC, which has now adopted a policy statement on homosexuals and the law. The same consultation revealed that the United Church Press wanted to publish a book on the issue, and so this volume got under way.

Ralph W. Weltge

sex
research

CHAPTER 1

Homosexuality

WARDELL B. POMEROY

There is probably more nonsense written about homosexuality, more unwarranted fear of it, and less understanding of it than of any other area of human sexuality. This brief chapter is an effort to bring more light than heat on the subject and to summarize at least some of the data available.

Homosexual behavior is defined as sexual activity between two persons of the same sex. It can consist of simple touching, kissing, petting, frictation, stroking the genitalia, mouth-genital contact, and anal intercourse (for the male). *Psychologic homosexual reactions* consist of an awareness of sexual arousal by seeing, hearing, or thinking about persons of the same sex. Such arousal is often accompanied by physiologic reactions such as deeper breathing, a warm skin, and tumescence.

In our society homosexuality has been variously considered to be unnatural, abnormal, inverted, perverted, immature, neurotic, psychopathic, and psychotic. There are stringent laws against it, and the three major churches in our country have historically condemned it. In recent years there have been reevaluations by

Dr. Wardell B. Pomeroy is a psychologist engaged in private practice as a marriage counselor in New York City. A graduate of Indiana University, he worked for twenty years on the staff of the Institute for Sex Research at that university, and served as the director of field research. He is the author of the recently published book *Boys and Sex.* Dr. Pomeroy is a coauthor of the pioneering volumes in the field of sex research: *Sexual Behavior in the Human Male; Sexual Behavior in the Human Female; Pregnancy, Birth, and Abortion;* and *Sex Offenders.*

This chapter is reprinted with revisions from Clark E. Vincent, *Human Sexuality in Medical Education and Practice,* 1968, by courtesy of Charles C. Thomas, Publisher, Springfield, Illinois.

some church groups, especially the Quakers, and now in this volume, by the United Church of Christ.

First, let us consider the "unnaturalness" of homosexual behavior. When we examine other species of mammals, we find homosexual activity, sometimes to the point of ejaculation, in all of the species studied. This is true of animals in the wild as well as animals in captivity. It is rare, however, for individual mammals to show an *exclusive* pattern of homosexual behavior. The majority have both heterosexual and homosexual activity, but heterosexual behavior predominates. Thus homosexual activity is "natural" in the sense that it occurs commonly in nature.[1] Instead of asking, "Why do human beings engage in homosexual behavior?" it is more meaningful to ask, "Why doesn't everyone engage in homosexual behavior?" inasmuch as it is part of our mammalian heritage. For the answer to this question we must turn to a consideration of our culture.

Attitudes Toward Homosexuality in Our Own Culture and in Other Societies

It is difficult for those who are not acquainted with cultures other than our own to understand fully how inhibited and rigid we are when it comes to sex. Anthropologists tell us that we are almost unique in the proscriptions, the anxieties, and the rigidities which we have developed in this area.[2]

A study of 193 world cultures,[3] for example, showed that 28 percent accepted male homosexuality and only 14 percent rejected it; in the remaining 58 percent, there was partial acceptance or some equivocation involved. As for female homosexuality, 10 percent accepted it, 11 percent rejected it, and there was partial acceptance or some equivocation in 79 percent. Homosexuality was even more widely accepted among 225 American Indian cultures. Some 53 percent of these cultures accepted male homosexuality and only 24 percent rejected it. Female homosexuality was accepted by 17 percent and it was rejected by 36 percent. Our own culture is plainly in the minority, not only in rejecting homosexuality but also in rejecting male homosexuality more forcibly than female homosexuality. Among the religions of the world, the Judeo-Christian system gives one of the harshest condemnations of homosexuality.

The past few years has seen a gradual but perceptible change toward greater openness in discussing various aspects of homosexuality. On television, radio, in the theater, in books and newspapers, there has been a flood of material on homosexuality. Don't forget that it was less than twenty years ago that the *New York Herald Tribune* broke the newspaper taboo about using the word masturbation in print. During the past twenty years a dozen or more homophile organizations such as the Mattachine, One, and the Daughters of Bilitis have begun to hold public meetings and publish magazines which can be bought on the newsstands. Only very recently one such organization was publicly given formal permission to operate as an approved club at Columbia University. Playwrights such as Tennessee Williams, James Baldwin, and Edward Albee have worked some homosexual themes into their plays and books. The Walter Jenkins scandal turned out to be a minor matter, and many persons publicly rose to Jenkins' defense.

The churches are now beginning to open up a dialogue on the subject, and many clergymen are openly stating that persons with active homosexual histories should be accepted into the brotherhood of the church. I would hope that this volume will have some influence in affecting the thinking of church members in this direction.

Homosexuality has been condemned more severely in this country than almost any other type of sexual behavior. In the 1950's Illinois became the first state (and up to the present time, the only state) to repeal the law against homosexual behavior occurring in private between consenting adults. Such acts can still be a felony in the other forty-nine states.

Our own legal system came to us from the English common law, which also decreed homosexual behavior to be a felony. In 1967 England changed its stand on the subject, and homosexual behavior between consenting adults in private is no longer against the law in England. Although it will take many decades, I am confident that all states in this country will eventually follow the lead of England and Illinois.

The abhorrence of homosexuality in England was derived from the ecclesiastic law. For many years after the signing of the Magna Charta in 1215, when the state wrested power from the church, the administration of sex laws was left in the hands of the church. When the state did finally take over the administration of these laws, it did not change the laws themselves.

The ecclesiastical laws on sex were derived from the talmudic law. This is understandable, since most of the early Christians were Jews. The talmudic laws on sex—including these on homosexuality—had been solidified after the Jews returned from the Babylonian exile in the fifth century *B.C.* Hence our own attitudes toward homosexuality can be traced in an unbroken line from present-day America to Judaism five centuries before Christ. Interestingly enough, the Jewish attitudes on homosexuality *before* the Babylonian exile were somewhat similar to those expressed in the present laws in England and Illinois. Homosexual behavior was allowed between peers but was prohibited if duress or seduction might be involved. Homosexual prostitution was actually part of the religious rites in the Jewish temples.

The Heterosexual-homosexual Continuum

In cultures that have no serious social sanctions against homosexual relations, males do not tend to develop an exclusive pattern of homosexuality, but, instead, combine homosexual and heterosexual activity. In our own culture a dichotomy is made between the two types of behavior, and often people are forced into deciding whether they are "homosexual" or "heterosexual." I recall a twenty-four-year-old single male patient of mine who announced that he was a homosexual. Inquiry revealed that he had had four overt homosexual experiences between the ages of fourteen and nineteen, and that he was slightly aroused by thinking about and seeing males. He also had dated many girls, had had intercourse with several of them, and was very much aroused by thinking of them and seeing them.

If we could break down this irrational concept of a dichotomy between heterosexuality and homosexuality, we might understand better how to help patients change in the direction of heterosexuality if that is their desire. The following diagram allows for five divisions in the continuum between exclusive heterosexuality (0) and exclusive homosexuality (6).

Individuals can be classified on this scale according to their overt behavior, their psychic response, or both. Ordinarily, overt behavior is closely related to psychologic reactions. When this is

HETEROSEXUAL-HOMOSEXUAL RATING SCALE

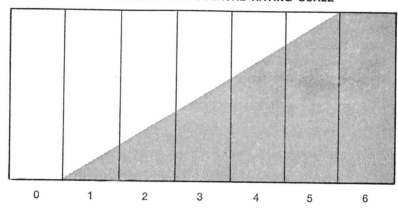

0 Exclusively heterosexual
1 Predominantly heterosexual, only incidentally homosexual
2 Predominantly heterosexual, but more than incidentally homosexual
3 Equally heterosexual and homosexual
4 Predominantly homosexual, but more than incidentally heterosexual
5 Predominantly homosexual, only incidentally heterosexual
6 Exclusively homosexual

not true—as, for example, in the case of a married man whose overt behavior would be classed as 2 (more heterosexual than homosexual), although his psychic response might be 4 (predominantly homosexual)—one can average the individual's ratings or can classify him on two different scales. Let me emphasize, however, that in most cases overt behavior follows psychologic response.

There is only a small likelihood that persons who have been in the 5 or 6 category on the rating scale for any appreciable period of time—five to ten years—will ever work down the scale, although homosexuals who are highly motivated to change may be able to do so. The important part to remember is that no matter where they stand on the scale, they cannot become more heterosexual by attempting to renounce or give up their homosexuality. The analogy I use is that one doesn't get to like ripe olives by giving up ice cream. The more one fights against homosexual desires, the larger they loom in one's consciousness. The positive approach is to attempt to get the patient to accept his homosexuality, even to the point of engaging in homosexual activities if he wants to, but at the same time to add something—namely, heterosexuality—to his sexual pattern. In order to do this, he must deliberately set out to meet girls, get to know them, and engage in gradual physical contact with them, until petting eventually leads to intercourse. If this process has the desired effect, the homosexual part of his life takes on less and less meaning until finally he can marry and work out a good marital adjustment. The homosexuality will still remain—usually in fantasy, although sometimes in overt practice—but it is no longer the compulsive, compelling drive that it was formerly. This procedure should be recommended only if the patient is highly motivated to become heterosexual; otherwise, the therapist should direct his effort toward helping the patient accept his homosexual life.

The Incidence of Homosexuality

Let me present some statistics that will give you an idea of the incidence of homosexual activity in this country.

1. About 37 percent of the males above the age of puberty have had at least one overt homosexual experience to the point of orgasm.

2. About 13 percent of the males react erotically to other males without having an overt experience after puberty.

3. About 13 percent of the females above the age of puberty have had at least one overt homosexual experience to the point of orgasm. Another 7 percent have had homosexual experience without orgasm.

4. About 8 percent of the females have had homosexual psychologic reactions without overt experience after puberty.

5. About 4 percent of the males and 2 to 3 percent of the females are exclusively homosexual throughout their lives.

6. Roughly 25 percent of the males and 10 percent of the females would be rated above *1* on the scale shown on page 7.

Even if these estimates are off by a wide margin, there is unquestionably a very considerable amount of homosexual activity and psychologic response in this country. Male homosexuality predominates, in spite of—or perhaps because of—the fact that overt expressions of affection between members of the same sex are more acceptable among women than among men. Women also appear to be able to change their position on the rating scale more easily than men. A man who rates in the *5* or *6* category on this scale for any appreciable time may eventually work his way down to a 2 rating with quite some effort. I have seen women change from a 6 to a 0 rating in a few months' time. This phenomenon seems to be related to the female's lesser ability to be sexually conditioned—a factor which shows up in many other sexual areas and accounts for one of the striking differences between males and females.

What Is "Latent" Homosexuality?

"Latent homosexuality" is a term that has been used rather loosely to express at least two concepts: (a) repressed homosexual desires which the person has not allowed to come into his consciousness, (b) psychologic homosexual reactions. According to the first concept, the latent homosexual desires continue to operate in a person's unconscious mind in such a manner as to cause conflict with his conscious heterosexuality. According to the second concept, a person who is aroused psychologically by seeing or thinking of someone of the same sex but does not have actual physical contact with such a person, is a "latent" homosexual. In this case, the desire is suppressed rather than repressed.

All of us have the potentiality of doing every criminal and antisocial act imaginable. Given the proper circumstances, the proper conditioning, and the proper background, we could murder, commit arson, be sadistic or masochistic, have intercourse with animals, or whatever. Thus one might say that we are all latent murderers, latent arsonists, and so forth. This concept is not a helpful one, however, unless we can understand what circumstances might lead us to overcome the restraints which prevent us from performing such acts. Since all of us, then, have latent homosexual tendencies to one degree or another, I do not believe the concept of latent homosexuality is a meaningful one. We are all latent millionaires also—but what of it?

Types of Homosexual Behavior

Just as there are many different degrees of homosexual behavior, there are also many different types of persons who engage in homosexual acts. Some persons—most often females—develop a long-standing emotional relationship with another person of the same sex and live with that person "monogamously" for periods ranging from a year to a lifetime. In some cases, the pair have no contact with other homosexuals; in other cases, they develop a coterie of friends who are living in similar circumstances. Such long-lasting homosexual relationships are more common in later years, after a period of promiscuity in the teens and twenties. They also occur more frequently at upper social levels than at lower levels.

Other homosexuals are promiscuous, flitting from one brief encounter to another (in homosexual parlance, "cruising"), and sometimes having several homosexual encounters in a single evening. In fact there are some males, known as "oncers," who will not have sexual experience twice with the same person. Obviously, such an individual will have literally thousands of different partners in the course of a lifetime.

Still other males have homosexual relations for money. Some cities have sections in which there are more male homosexual prostitutes than female heterosexual prostitutes. Many of the males enter this life in their teens and early twenties for a short time, and then drop out and return to a completely heterosexual life. Some go into robbery and burglary and others become customers for other male prostitutes. Whereas in female prostitution it is the paying customer who ejaculates, the customer of the male prostitute pays for the privilege of bringing him to an ejaculation.

Some males begin homosexual activity as a result of being confined to an all-male environment, such as a prison or other institution. Usually such persons, if previously heterosexual, return to a heterosexual life after release from confinement. In other situations a person may have an incidental homosexual experience while drinking or when a partner of the opposite sex is not immediately available.

From this brief description of the many types of homosexual patterns, it is obvious that to lump all homosexuals together is as grossly misleading as to lump all heterosexuals together. Homosexuality is no respecter of age, religion, or social level. It occurs as frequently among physicians, psychiatrists, clergymen, judges, and politicians as among truck drivers and ditch diggers.

Myths Surrounding Homosexuality

The common myth that homosexual males are effeminate and identifiable and that homosexual females are swaggering, "butch" types is not borne out by the facts. About 15 percent of the males and 5 percent of the females with extensive homosexual histories are identifiable. The others are able to live in society without attracting undue notice. To confuse the picture further, there are a few "false positives"—people whose mannerisms, vocal inflections, or way of dress suggests homosexuality even though they have no homosexual tendencies.

The relation between effeminacy and homosexuality is most elusive. Overt homosexual contact was probably more common among the cowboys and the Indian fighters of the West in the nineteenth century than among any other single group of males in our country. Although they despised the effeminate man, they were quite acceptant of homosexual activity. The high concentration of persons with homosexual histories in both fine arts and applied arts is not due, as many believe, to a "softness" or effeminacy which attracts them to such pursuits. Among the real factors are the wider acceptance of homosexuals in these fields, the greater freedom to express themselves, and the greater uncertainty about the future, which they can tolerate more easily than a married man with a family.

Another myth about homosexuality is that the homosexual is likely to be a child molester or at least a seducer of young children. In many states a male convicted of a homosexual offense is not allowed to teach school, the theory being that it would be dangerous to expose young boys to his malevolent influence. Little thought is given to the dangers of exposing young girls to the malevolent influence of heterosexual teachers. The assumption seems to be that the latter are better able to control their pedophilic tendencies. The facts do not warrant such fears. The great majority of homosexual males have no more sexual interest in young boys than the great majority of heterosexual males have in young girls. An undetermined but sizable proportion of the pedophiles are sexually attracted to young children per se, regardless of their gender.

Etiology of Homosexuality

The etiology of homosexuality is still poorly understood, but it is very doubtful that one single factor will be found to account for this phenomenon. Some workers in this field believe there is a genetic factor in homosexuality. If it is accepted that humans, being mammals, have a genetic structure in which homosexuality is ubiquitous, one would need to show that some *individual* human beings have received more of this genetic factor than others. In his study on twins,[4] Kallman showed that all forty of the co-twins of his monozygotic homosexual subjects were homosexual, whereas less than half of the co-twins of his dizygotic homosexual subjects were homosexual. Among the criticisms that have been made of this study are the fact that most of the subjects were schizophrenic or otherwise emotionally upset, that only one set of twins was found to have a homosexual father, and that the author did not define how homosexual a person had to be in order to be classified as "homosexual." More recent studies of monozygotic twins have shown several cases in which one of the pair was homosexual, and the other heterosexual.

Hormonal studies have proven almost uniformly negative in eliciting differences between homosexual and heterosexual individuals, as have studies of body build, genital anatomy, and brain injuries. Studies showing any positive findings in these areas have been poorly done, have had too few subjects or a selection of subjects, or have been contradicted by other studies.

Freud developed the concept that homosexuality is a stage of psychosexual growth which occurs, typically, near puberty and precedes heterosexuality. According to this concept, nearly everyone goes through this stage—in fact, it is a necessary part of growing up. Some become fixated at this level and never develop beyond it. Others become fixated at still lower levels, such as the narcissistic stage, and never grow into the homosexual stage. Although such a concept is difficult to prove or disprove, the data that have been garnered would indicate that people do not necessarily pass through these phases of psychosexual growth. Certainly when we look at overt behavior we find that the onset and practice of masturbation, homosexuality, and heterosexuality may occur in any order.

Most workers in this area now lean toward a conditioning theory, although they acknowledge that physical characteristics or other predisposing factors *indirectly* play a part in the development of a homosexual pattern. As an illustration, a boy who is physically weak or uncoordinated and is shunned or laughed at by his peers may have an early homosexual experience which gives him the acceptance by a male that he longs for. Hence he may be strongly conditioned toward homosexual activity by an experience that another boy, less in need of acceptance, might toss off with few aftereffects. Numerous other examples could be given to show how predisposing factors, either physical or psychologic, make it easy for a homosexual experience to become of tremendous importance to an individual.

It can be seen from the example just given that homosexuality can develop from a series of negative reasons as well as positive ones. A male (or female) may feel so shy, timid, anxious, fearful, rejected, or hostile toward the opposite sex that he is unable to have any sociosexual experience at all, except with members of his own sex. Hence homosexuality can develop by default, or because of a lack of heterosexuality.

Is Homosexuality an Illness or a Way of Life?

A controversy now exists as to whether homosexuality should be considered an "illness" (an emotional disturbance) or a choice—an acceptable way of life. Some clinicians have insisted that all homosexuals are neurotic, if not psychotic, and that they will inevitably be better off if they are "cured" of their homosexual tendencies.

If my concept of homosexuality were developed from my practice, I would probably concur in thinking of it as an illness. I have seen no homosexual man or woman in that practice who was not troubled, emotionally upset, or neurotic. On the other hand, if my concept of marriage in the United States were based on my practice, I would have to conclude that marriages are all fraught with strife and conflict, and that heterosexuality is an illness. In my twenty years of research in the field of sex, I have seen many homosexuals who were happy, who were participating and conscientious members of their community, and who were stable, productive, warm, relaxed, and efficient. Except for the fact that they were homosexual, they would be considered normal by any definition. To insist that they are abnormal, or sick, or neurotic just because they are homosexual is to engage in circular reasoning which smacks of a blind moralism founded in our Judeo-Christian heritage.

CHAPTER 2

Homosexuality: The Formulation of a Sociological Perspective

WILLIAM SIMON AND JOHN H. GAGNON

The study of homosexuality today, except for a few rare and relatively recent examples, suffers from two major defects: (1) It is ruled by a simplistic and homogeneous view of the psychological and social contents of the category "homosexual." (2) At the same time it is nearly exclusively interested in the most difficult and least rewarding of all questions, that of etiology. While some small exclusions are allowed for adolescent homosexual experimentation, the person with a major to a nearly exclusive sexual interest in persons of the same sex is perceived as belonging to a uniform category whose adult behavior is a necessary outcome and, in a sense, reenactment, of certain early and determining experiences. This is the prevailing image of the homosexual and the substantive concern of the literature in psychiatry and psychology today.

In addition to the fact that sexual contact with persons of the same sex, even beyond the age of consent, is against the law in forty-nine of the fifty state jurisdictions of the United States, the

---

Dr. William Simon is program director in sociology and anthropology at the Institute for Juvenile Research in Chicago. Dr. John H. Gagnon is associate professor of sociology at the State University of New York at Stony Brook. Formerly both were senior research sociologists at the Institute for Sex Research of Indiana University. They co-edited the book *Sexual Deviance.* Together they have published numerous articles in professional and popular journals, and have a continuing interest in urban youth, particularly their problems with sex and drugs.

This chapter is reprinted with revisions from *Journal of Health and Social Behavior,* Vol. VIII, No. 3 (September 1967), by courtesy of the American Sociological Society.

homosexual labors under another burden which is commonly the lot of the deviant in this society. The process of labeling and stigmatizing behavior not only facilitates the work of legal agencies in creating a bounded category of deviant actors such as the "normal burglar" and the "normal child molester" as suggested by Sudnow, but also creates an image of large classes of deviant actors all operating out of the same motivations and for the same etiological reasons. The homosexual, like most significantly labeled persons (whether the label be positive or negative), has all of his acts interpreted through the framework of his homosexuality. Thus the creative activity of the playwright or painter who happens to be homosexual is interpreted in terms of his homosexuality rather than in terms of the larger artistic rules and conventions of the particular art form in which he works. The plays of the dramatist are scanned for the Albertine Ploy and the painter's paintings for an excessive or deficient use of phallic imagery or vaginal teeth.

It is this nearly obsessive concern with the ultimate causes of adult conditions which has played a major role in structuring our concerns about beliefs and about attitudes toward the homosexual. Whatever the specific elements that make up an etiological theory, the search for etiology has its own consequences for research methodology and the construction of theories about behavior. In the case of homosexuality, if one moves beyond those explanations of homosexual behavior which are rooted in constitutional or biological characteristics—that is, something in the genes or in the hormonal system—one is left with etiological explanations located in the structure of the family and its malfunctions. The most compelling of these theories are grounded ultimately in Freudian psychology, where the roots of this behavior as well as the rest of human character structure are to be found in the pathological relationships between parents and their children.[1]

As a consequence of our preliminary work and the work of others such as Hooker, Reiss, Leznoff and Westley, and Achilles, we would like to propose some alternative considerations in terms of the complexity of the life cycle of the homosexual, the roles that mark various stages of this cycle, and the kinds of forces, both sexual and nonsexual, that impinge on the individual actor. It is our current feeling that the problem of finding out how people become homosexual requires an adequate theory of how they become heterosexual; that is, one cannot explain homosexuality in one way and leave heterosexuality as a large residual category labeled "all other." Indeed, the explanation of homosexuality in this sense may await the explanation of the larger and more modal category of adjustment.

Further, from a sociological point of view, what the original causes were may not even be very important for the patterns of homosexuality observed in a society. Much like the medical student who comes to medicine for many reasons, and for whom the homogeneity that is professional behavior arises from the experiences of medical school rather than from the root causes of his occupational choice, the patterns of adult homosexuality are attendant upon the social structures and values which occur to the homosexual after he becomes, or conceives of himself as, homosexual, rather than upon original and ultimate causes.

What we are suggesting here is that we have allowed the sexual object choice of the homosexual to dominate and control our imagery and have let this aspect of his total life experience appear to determine all his products, concerns, and activities. This prepossessing concern on the part of non-homosexuals with the purely sexual aspect of the homosexual's life is something which we would not allow to occur if we were interested in the heterosexual, but the mere presence of sexual deviation seems to give the sexual content of life an overwhelming significance. Homosexuals, moreover, vary profoundly in the degree to which their homosexual commitment and its facilitation becomes the organization principle of their lives. Involved is a complex outcome which is less likely to be explained by originating circumstances than by the consequences of the establishment of the commitment itself.

Even with the relatively recent shift in the normative framework available for considering homosexuality—that is, from a rhetoric of sin to a rhetoric of mental health—the overweighting of the sexual factor is evident. The change itself may have major significance in the ways in which homosexual persons are dealt with; at the same time, the mental health rhetoric seems equally wide of the mark in understanding homosexuality. One advance, however, is that in place of the language of optimum man which characterized both the moral and the early mental health literature, we find a growing literature concerned with what are the psychological characteristics necessary for a person to survive in some manner within specific social systems and social situations. In this post-Freudian world, major psychic wounds are increasingly viewed as par for the human condition and—as one major psychiatric theoretician observes—few survive their parents without such wounding. The problem then becomes whether the wounds inflicted are exposed to social situations which render them either too costly to the individual or to the surrounding community.

Accompanying this trend toward reconceptualization of mental health has been a scaling down of the goals set for men; instead of exceedingly vague and somewhat utopian goals, we tend to ask more pragmatic questions: Is the individual self-supporting? Does he manage to conduct his affairs without the intervention of the police or the growing number of mental health authorities? Does he have adequate sources of social support? a positively balanced and adequately developed repertoire of gratification? Has he learned to accept himself? These are questions we are learning to ask of nearly all men; among the remaining exceptions is found the homosexual. In practically all cases, the presence of homosexuality is seen as prima facie evidence of major psychopathology. When the heterosexual meets these minimal definitions of mental health, he is exculpated; the homosexual—no matter how good his adjustment in nonsexual areas of life is—remains suspect.

Our own recently tabulated data, drawn from homosexuals interviewed outside of institutions, suggest that most homosexuals manage fairly well and particularly well when we consider the stigmatized and, in fact, criminal nature of their sexual interests. In a group of homosexuals with extensive histories of homosexuality, we found that about 80 percent reported no trouble with the police and an additional 10 percent had had minor contacts but were not arrested. Only 20 percent reported problems of managing relations with their parental families, and about 10 percent or under reported difficulties in school or work. Of those who had had military experience, only one fifth reported difficulties. And with reference to the military, it is important to note that in the military, possibly more than in civilian life, homosexuality is a difficulty which washes out all other considerations.

We do not want to appear to be saying that the homosexual life does not contain a great potential for demoralization, despair, and self-hatred. To the contrary, as in most deviant careers there remains the potential for a significant escalation of individual psychopathology. This also is suggested by other segments of these same data. For example, we found that over two fifths indicated some measure of regret about being homosexual, giving reasons such as fear of social disapproval or rejection, inability to experience a conventional family life, feelings of guilt and shame, or fear of potential trouble. About one half reported that 50 percent or more of their sexual partners were persons with whom the subject had had only one contact (one-night stand), and for about one quarter this was true for 80 percent or more of their contacts. For two fifths, their longest homosexual affair had lasted one year or less. For about one quarter, kissing occurred in one third or less of all their sexual contacts. About 30 percent had never made love in their own homes. To this we should add the proportion of homosexuals who report having been robbed (frequently after being beaten)—over 25 percent—and the proportion who have been blackmailed—almost 10 percent. These figures require more detailed analysis and there are also uncertainties about sample bias which must be considered. However, it is our feeling that these proportions would not be changed a great deal given a more complete exploration of these factors. These data, then, suggest a depersonalized quality, a driven or compulsive quality, to the sexual activity of many homosexuals, which cannot be reckoned as anything but extremely costly to them.

Obviously, the pursuit of a homosexual commitment—like most forms of deviance—makes social adjustment more problematic than it might be for a conventional population. What is important to understand is that consequences of these sexual practices are not necessarily direct functions of such practices. It is necessary to move away from an obsessive concern with the sexuality of the individual, and to attempt to see the homosexual in terms of broader commitments that he must make in order to live in the world around him. Like the heterosexual, the homosexual must come to terms with the problems which are attendant upon being a member of the society: he must find a place to work, learn to live with or without his family, be involved or apathetic in political life, find a group of friends to talk to and live with, fill his leisure time usefully or frivolously, handle all of the common and uncommon problems of impulse control and personal gratification, and in some manner socialize his sexual interests.

There is a nearly unnoticed diversity to be found in the life cycle of the homosexual, both in terms of solving common human problems and in terms of the characteristics of the life cycle itself. Not only are there as many ways of being homosexual as there are of being heterosexual but the individual homosexual in the course of living his life encounters as many changes and as many crises as the heterosexual. It is much too easy to allow the label, once applied, to suggest that the complexities of role transition and identity crisis are easily attributable to, or are a crucial exemplification of, some previously existing etiological defect.

An example of this is in the phase of homosexuality called "coming out," which is that point in time when there is self-recognition of one's identity as a homosexual and the first major entry into exploration of the homosexual community. At this point in time, the removal of inhibiting doubts frequently releases a great deal of sexual energy. Sexual contacts during this period are often pursued nearly indiscriminately and with greater vigor than caution. This is very close to that period in the life of the heterosexual called the "honeymoon," when coitus is legitimate and is pursued with a substantial amount of energy. This high rate of marital coitus, however, declines as demands are made on the young couple to take their place in the framework of the larger social system. In these same terms, during the homosexual honeymoon many individuals begin to learn ways of acting out a homosexual object choice which involves homosexual gratification, but which is not necessarily directly sexual and does not involve the genitalia.

It is during this period that many homosexuals go through a crisis of femininity; that is, they act in relatively public places in a relatively effeminate manner and some, in a transitory fashion, wear female clothing—known in the homosexual argot as going in drag. During this period, one of the major confirming aspects of masculinity—that is, nonsexual reinforcement by females of masculine status—has been abandoned, and it is not surprising that the very core of masculine identity should not be called into question. This crisis is partially structured by the already existing homosexual culture in which persons already in the crisis stage become models for those who are newer to their commitment to homosexuality. A few males remain in this commitment to pseudo-femininity, a few others emerge masquerading as female prostitutes to males, and still others pursue careers as female impersonators. This adjustment might be more widely adapted if feminine behavior by men—except in sharply delimited occupational roles—were not negatively sanctioned. The tendency is, then, for this kind of behavior to be a transitional experiment for most homosexuals—an experiment that leaves vestiges of "camp" behavior, but vestiges more often expressive of the character of the cultural life of the homosexual community than of some overriding need of individual homosexuals. Since this period of disorganization and identity problems is at the same time highly visible to the broader community, this femininity is enlisted as evidence for theories of homosexuality that see as a central component in its etiology the failure of sexual identification. The homosexual at this point of the life cycle is more likely to be in therapy, and this is often construed as evidence for a theory which is supported by a missampling of the ways of being homosexual.

Another life-cycle crisis that the homosexual shares with the heterosexual in this youth-oriented society is the crisis of aging. While American society places an inordinate emphasis on youth as a positive attribute, the homosexual community, by and large, places a still greater emphasis on this fleeting characteristic. In general, the homosexual has fewer resources with which to meet this crisis. For the heterosexual there are children whose careers assure a sense of the future, and a wife whose sexual availability cushions the shock of declining sexual attractiveness. In addition, the crisis of aging comes later to the heterosexual when sexual powers have declined and expectations concerning sexuality are considerably lower. The management of aging by the homosexual is not well understood but there are, at this point in time, a series of behavioral manifestations—symptoms—attendant to this dramatic transition which are misread as global aspects of homosexuality. Here, as with coming out, it is important to note that most homosexuals, even with fewer resources than their heterosexual counterparts, manage to weather the period with relative success.

A central concern underlying these options and the management of a homosexual career is the presence and complexity of a homosexual community which serves most simply for some persons as a sexual marketplace, but for others as the locus of friendships, opportunities, recreation, and expansion of the base of social life. Such a community is filled with both formal and informal institutions for meeting others and for following, to the degree the individual wants, a homosexual life style. Minimally the community provides a source of social support, for it is one of the few places where the homosexual may get positive validation of his own self-image. Though the community often provides more feminine or camp behavior than some individuals might desire, in a major sense camp behavior may well be an expression of the aggregate community characteristics without an equal commitment on the part of its members. Further, the camp behavior may also be seen as a form of interpersonal communication that characterizes persons during intra-community behavior and changes significantly for most during interaction with the larger society. The community serves as a way of mediating sexuality by providing a situation in which one can know and evaluate peers and, in a significant sense, convert sexual behavior into sexual conduct.

Insofar as the community provides these relationships for the individual homosexual, it allows for the dilution of sexual drives by providing social gratification in ways which are not directly sexual, and in consequence the homosexual with access to the community is more protected from impulsive sexual acting out than the homosexual who has only his fear and his knowledge of the society's prohibitions to mediate his sexual impulses.

It should be pointed out that in contrast to ethnic and occupational subcultures the homosexual community—as well as other deviant subcommunities—has very limited content. This derives from the fact that the community members often have only their sexual commitment in common. Thus, while the community may reduce the problems of access to sexual partners and reduce guilt by providing a structure of shared values, often the shared value structure of the community is far too narrow to transcend other areas of value disagreement. The college-trained professional and the busboy, the WASP and the Negro slum dweller may meet in a sexual congress, but the similarity of their sexual interests does not eliminate the larger social and cultural barriers.[2] The important fact is that the homosexual community is, in itself, an impoverished cultural unit. This impoverishment, however, may only be partially limiting, since it constrains most members to participate in it on a limited basis, thereby reducing anxiety and conflicts in the sexual sphere and increasing the quality of performance in other aspects of social life.

Earlier we briefly listed some of the general problems that the homosexual—in common with the heterosexual—must face; these included earning a living, maintaining a residence, learning to live with family. At this point, we might consider some of these in greater detail.

First there is the most basic problem of all: earning a living. Initially, all the variables that apply to all labor force participants generally also apply to homosexuals. In addition there are the special conditions imposed by the deviant character of the homosexual commitment. What is important is that the occupational activity of homosexuals presents itself as a fairly broad range. The differences in occupational activity can be conceptualized along a number of dimensions—some of which would be conventional concerns of occupational sociology, while others would reflect the special situation of the homosexual. For example, one element would be the degree of occupational involvement; that is, the degree to which occupational activity or ancillary activity is defined as intrinsically gratifying. This would obviously vary from professional to ribbon clerk to factory laborer. A corollary to this would be the degree to which the world of work penetrates other aspects of life. The first of these elements—involvement—is important if only as part of a consideration of alternative sources of gratification available. In terms of influence upon a homosexual career, involvement very likely plays a constraining role during the acting-out phase associated with coming out, as well as serving as a source of alternative investment during the "crisis of aging." The second bears directly upon the issue of the consequences of having one's deviant commitment exposed. For some occupational roles disclosure would clearly be a disaster—the schoolteacher, the minister, the politician, to mention just three. There are other occupations where the disclosure or assumption of homosexual interests is either of little consequence or—though a relatively few—where it has a positive consequence. It should be evident that the crucial question of anxiety and depersonalization in the conduct of sexual activity can be linked to this variable in a rather direct way.

A second series of questions could deal with the effects of a deviant sexual commitment upon occupational activity itself. In some cases the effect may be extremely negative as pursuit of homosexual goals may generate irresponsibility and irregularity. Some part of this might flow from what we associate with bachelorhood generally: detachment from social structure and, on the sexual level, constant striving for what is essentially regularized in marriage. More simply stated this would be: too many late nights out, too much drinking in too many taverns, and unevenness in emotional condition. On the other hand, several positive effects can be observed. Detachment from the demands of domestic life not only frees one for greater dedication to the pursuit of sexual goals, but also for greater dedication to work. Also, the ability of some jobs to facilitate homosexual activity—such as certain marginal, low-paying white-collar jobs—serves as compensation for low pay or limited opportunity for advancement. There may be few simple or consistent patterns emerging from this type of consideration, yet the overdetermination of the sexual in the study of the homosexual rests in our prior reluctance to consider these questions which are both complex and pedestrian.

Similarly, just as most homosexuals have to earn a living, so must they come to terms with their immediate families. There is no substantial evidence to suggest that the proportion of homosexuals for whom relatives are significant persons differs from that of heterosexuals. The important differences rest in the way the relationships are managed and, again, the consequences they have for other aspects of life. Here also, one could expect considerable variation containing patterns of rejection, continuing involvement without knowledge, ritualistically suppressed knowledge, and knowledge and acceptance. This becomes more complex as several of the patterns may be operative at the same time with different members of one's family constellation. Here again it is not unreasonable to assume a considerable degree of variation in the course of managing a homosexual commitment as this kind of factor varies. Yet the literature is almost totally without reference to these relationships. Curiously, in the psychiatric literature—where mother and father play crucial roles in the formation of a homosexual commitment—they tend to be significant by their absence in considerations of how homosexual lives are lived.

This order of discussion could be extended into a large number of areas. Let us consider just one more: religion. As a variable, religion (as both an identification and a quality of religiousness) manifests no indication that it plays an important role in the generation of homosexual commitments. Clearly, it does or can play a significant role in the management of that commitment. Here, as in other spheres of life, we must be prepared to deal with complex, interactive relations rather than fixed, static ones. Crucial to the homosexual's ability to "accept himself" is his ability to bring his own homosexuality within a sense of the moral order as it is projected by the institutions surrounding him as well as his own vision of this order. It may be that the question of bringing homosexuality within a religious definition is the way the question should be framed only part of the time, and for only part of a homosexual population. At other times—for other homosexuals —to frame the question in terms of bringing religiousness within the homosexual definition might be more appropriate. The need for damnation—that rare sense of being genuinely evil—and the need for redemption—a sense of potentially being returned to the community in good standing—can be expected to vary given different stages of the life cycle, given different styles of being homosexual, given varying environments within which the homosexual commitment is to be enacted. And our sense of the relation suggests that more than asking of the homosexual's religious production, how it expresses his homosexuality, we must also learn to ask how his homosexuality expresses his commitment to the religious.

The aims, then, of a sociological approach to homosexuality are to begin to define the factors—both individual and situational —that predispose a homosexual to follow one homosexual path as against others; to spell out the contingencies which will shape the career that has been embarked upon; to trace out the patterns of living in their pedestrian aspects as well as those which are seemingly exotic. Only then will we begin to understand the homosexual, and this pursuit must inevitably bring us—though from a particular angle—to those complex matrices wherein most human behavior is fashioned.

CHAPTER 3

The Homosexual Community

EVELYN HOOKER

In view of its socially tabooed character, it is not difficult to understand why homosexuality as a collective phenomenon in urban settings has rarely been subjected to scientific investigation.[1] The necessity of escaping the penalties of social or legal recognition impels many homosexuals to lead a highly secret private life. Only when caught by law enforcement agents, or when seeking psychiatric help, are they usually available for study. Gaining access to secret worlds of homosexuals, and maintaining rapport while conducting an ethnographic field study, requires the development of a non-evaluative attitude toward all forms of sexual behavior. Social scientists tend to share the emotional attitudes of their culture, and thus do not find this an easy task. Most psychological studies of homosexuality are clinical in orientation and largely concerned with individual psychodynamics.[2] I know of only one sociological study of a homosexual community in an urban setting (Leznoff & Westley, 1956).

The present investigation of the homosexual community in metropolitan Los Angeles is part of a large project, on which I have been engaged for seven years, which also includes a study of the multiple developmental routes by which males travel to self-indentification as homosexuals, and an analysis of adult per-

Dr. Evelyn Hooker is a research psychologist at the University of California in Los Angeles. Since 1954 she has been engaged in the study of homosexuals in the context of the homosexual community. Her research has been supported by the National Institute of Mental Health, the United States Public Health Service.

This chapter is reprinted with the permission of the author and publishers from *Perspectives in Psychopathology* (New York: Oxford University Press, 1965). It first appeared in the *Proceedings of the XIV International Congress of Applied Psychology* (Copenhagen: Munksgaard, 1961).

sonality structure and adjustment (Hooker, 1956, 1957, 1958, 1959). It has become increasingly clear that these aspects of the problem must be viewed as functionally interrelated: the homosexual community or world and the kinds of persons who travel those paths and live in that world cannot be treated as independent of each other. The relations between personality variables and homosexual subculture variables in determining the commitment to, and patterns of, adult homosexuality are complex. For many, the stability of the commitment appears to be a function of the interaction of both sets of variables.

My methods of studying the homosexual community are essentially those of an ethnographer: interviewing its members about the institutions and activities, and participating in those activities whenever possible, with subsequent recording of my observations. Full participation is impossible for two reasons: my gender —I am studying a male community [3]—and my research role. My objective is to see the homosexual world through the eyes of research subjects as the only way in which to know what is really going on, to look with the subject at his world as he knows it. Only if I can achieve and maintain an attitude such that non-evaluation is constant, and that whatsoever I hear or see is simply a matter of sheer interest, will I be able to establish the necessary conditions of trust for complete frankness. The homosexual mask in the presence of a representative of the dominant culture is so firmly set, the expectation of moral disapproval so constant, and the distrust and suspicion of motives so ready to be alerted, that the researcher must prove his trustworthiness again and again. Only if the genuineness of the researcher's interest in simply understanding what he sees and hears is conveyed by his total attitudes of feeling and behavior, is it possible to enlist the full cooperation of the subjects. They must become, in effect, research assistants in the enterprise, seeking to learn as much for themselves about the community in which they live as for the researcher, and to enlist others as well.

My original access to the community was not deliberately sought for research purposes, but developed quite accidentally in the course of normal processes of social interaction with a group of friends to whom I had been introduced by a former student—a highly successful businessman. After a period of testing my capacity to accept their behavior in a non-judgmental way, while divesting themselves of their protective masks, they made an urgent request that I conduct a scientific investigation of "people like them." By people like them, they meant homosexuals who did not seek psychiatric help, and who led relatively stable, occupationally successful lives. They had read clinical literature on homosexuality and felt that much of it was irrelevant to an understanding of their condition. With their offer to supply unlimited numbers of research subjects, and to provide entrée into homosexual circles and public gathering places, I accepted the research opportunity. Thus, the original relationship was not that of researcher to research subject, but of friend to friend. With the expansion of contacts through networks of mutual friends, the research role became more clearly defined and separated from its social origin. Independent contacts with official homosexual organizations led to other social strata in the community. Participation in the community and deliberate efforts to locate representative members of varying sectors of it, such as male prostitutes, bisexuals, bartenders and bar owners, adolescents and the aged, produced ultimately a wide cross section.

There are no unique features of Los Angeles which are necessary conditions for the development of a homosexual community since one exists in every large city in the United States, and indeed, probably in the Western world. Only the roughest estimates can be made of the numbers of practicing homosexuals in Los Angeles. The Kinsey estimates of 4 percent of the white male population as being exclusively homosexual throughout their lives would give an approximate figure of 26,631, age twenty or over, on the basis of the 1960 census. Exclusive homosexuals, however, account for a small proportion of the total. If we accept the Kinsey estimates, the incidence of those having some overt homosexual experience between adolescence and old age reaches 37 percent. The largest proportion will have had heterosexual experiences as well. Thus, the suggested figure does not even begin to encompass the total white homosexual population in Los Angeles—to say nothing of non-Caucasians of whom there are many.

That portion of the homosexual population which forms a loosely organized society, world, or collectivity having a unified character, as distinguished from a mere aggregate of persons, is not a community in the traditional sense of the term, as it has been used by sociologists, in that it lacks a territorial base with primary institutions serving a residential population. If, however, one is permitted to use the term to refer to an aggregate of persons engaging in common activities, sharing common interests, and having a feeling of sociopsychological unity, with variations in the degree to which persons have these characteristics, depending on whether they constitute the core or the periphery,[4] then it is completely germane to homosexuals. Although homosexuals as a total group do not have a bounded territorial base, they are nevertheless not randomly distributed throughout the city, nor are the facilities of institutions which provide needed services and functions as focal gathering places. Mapping the residences of persons known to us, or known to subjects who have supplied us with their addresses, and noting the residential areas in the city described by them as having heavy concentrations of homosexuals results in large cluster formations. In these sections, apartment houses on particular streets may be owned by, and rented exclusively to, homosexuals. Single streets of individual dwellings may have only one or two non-homosexual families. The concentrated character of these areas is not generally known except in the homosexual community, and in many instances by the police. The population is also distributed widely throughout the city and its suburbs since other factors than association affect the choice of residence. Buying of tract houses by "married pairs" has become sufficiently common [so areas are] referred to as "homosexual suburbia," the term referring to style of living and not the character of the neighborhood.

An adequate description of the "gay life"—that is, the homosexual community life or "scene" as the member knows it—depends on whether it satisfies the conditions of our being able to tell a person how to act, think, and feel as the homosexual does as he "makes the scene." [5] That scene, as the community member knows it, is essentially a round of activities utilizing a particular set of institutions, facilities, or areas and governed by common expectations, beliefs, and values. It is important to distinguish between the visible or public community activities in which only a small portion of the total homosexual population appears to participate, and the invisible, private community activities which go on in friendship cliques. A commonplace, but relevant, analogy is the iceberg in which only the top of a very large mass is visible. A stranger to the community may enter it via its public institutions, provided he knows where they are, or its private clique structure, provided he can manage a social introduction. Experienced homosexuals who are strangers to a particular community have no difficulty using either entrance since the community map is fairly standard from one city to another in the United States. The most favorable entrance for the researcher is via the clique structure since it leads inevitably to the public community, whereas the reverse is more difficult.

In the present account of the community, however, I shall begin with the public institutions, facilities, and areas used by homosexuals in their round of activities. Because most homosexuals make every effort to conceal their homosexuality at work, and from heterosexuals, the community activities are largely leisure-time or recreational activities. The most important of these community gathering places is the "gay" bar ("gay" is a synonym for "homosexual" as used by members of that community), but there are also steam baths catering almost exclusively to homosexuals, gay streets, parks, public toilets, beaches, gyms, coffeehouses, and restaurants. Newsstands, bookstores, record shops, clothing stores, barber shops, grocery stores, and launderettes may become preferred establishments for service or for a rendezvous, but they are secondary in importance.

In the Los Angeles area, there are at present count, sixty gay bars. Since their continued operation is subject to surveillance by police and alcoholic beverage control authorities, it is difficult to keep the list current. They are not randomly distributed over the city even in areas which permit the licensing of establishments for the dispensing of liquor. A map of the city on which the locations of gay bars is plotted shows that, like the residential areas, there is a clustering effect. Bars tend to be grouped in a given area in part because of the bar-going habits of their clientele. An individual seldom spends an entire evening in a particular bar, but usually makes the rounds of bars in a particular area, going from one bar to another, seeking sexual contacts or social partners. There is, therefore, a large turnover of personnel in a given evening. Bars nearby can capitalize on this fact. The areas in which the clusters of bars occur in Los Angeles are characterized by proximity to one or more of the following places: (1) residential areas with heavy concentrations of homosexuals, (2) beaches or other places of homosexual group recreation or leisure-time activity, (3) public entertainment districts—theaters, etc., (4) areas of high tolerance for and relative permissiveness toward other forms of deviant behavior. In Los Angeles there are five regions in which gay bars are located. The location of any given bar, however, within a general region depends on multiple factors too complex for elaboration in this presentation.

I begin the account of the community life with gay bars for a number of reasons: (1) In them, the public aspect of gay life is to be encountered—any stranger may enter. (2) Here, the gay and "straight" (heterosexual) worlds intersect: the gay world can become most visible to the straight world or to representatives of the straight world—the police, newspapers, etc. (3) On behalf of these institutions in the gay world, the legitimacy claim is most often made by protagonists such as lawyers in the straight world. (4) Here, one will find the largest and widest representation of types, socioeconomic levels, and social strata in the homosexual world—if one goes from bar to bar, as the homosexual does. It is estimated that on a Saturday night between the hours of 10:00 and 2:00 a.m., a thousand men will pass through the doors of one of the largest and most successful bars. (5) Here, one may observe one of the most standardized and characteristic patterns of social interaction in the gay world: the meeting of strangers for the essential purpose of making an agreement to engage in sexual activity known as the "one night stand." (6) For many homosexuals the gay bar is a social institution, where friends are met, the news of the homosexual world is to be heard, gossip exchanged, invitations to parties issued, and warnings about current danger spots and attitudes of the police given.

I conceive of homosexual bars as free markets which could only arise under a market economy in which buyers and sellers are governed by rules whereby the right to enter in is determined by whether the buyer has the wherewithal. The term market as applied to bars has two meanings: (1) a business enterprise in which leisure is accomplished via the market—gain from the sale of liquor and entertainment is legitimate, (2) a metaphor to conceive of transactions between homosexuals, a set of terms relating to the negotiation of an exchange of sexual services.

While individual bars are relatively unstable and may be short-lived, the bar system is relatively stable, although subject to the constant surveillance of appropriate authorities of the repressive agencies. Its stability may be accounted for by the following facts: (1) Bars are highly lucrative for the owners and despite harassment and closing of individual bars, licenses are constantly sought to reopen under new ownership or to establish ones in new locations. (2) They meet the expectations and needs, and are geared in an integral way to the behavior patterns of a large homosexual population. (3) Authorities unofficially believe that elimination of the system is both undesirable and impossible: "that kind of person has to have someplace to go and at least they are with their own kind, and you don't lose 'em; you just move 'em around a little."

The successful operation of a gay bar is a highly skilled performance requiring a knowledge of tastes and behavior of homosexual clientele, and the ability to create the kind of atmosphere which will attract large numbers, as well as the ability to successfully control behavior within the limits which law enforcement officers, behaving as willing objects of the cruising game, and thus passing as ordinary clientele, cannot make the subject of legal objection.

I turn now to the second meaning of the term market as applied to gay bars; that is, as a sexual market: a place where agreements are made for the potential exchange of sexual services, for sex without obligation or commitment—the "one night stand." If one watches very carefully, and knows what to watch for in a gay bar, one observes that some individuals are apparently communicating with each other without exchanging words, but simply by exchanging glances—but not the kind of quick glance which ordinarily occurs between men. It is said by homosexuals that if another catches and holds the glance, one need know nothing more about him to know that he is one of them. The psychological structure of that meeting of glances is a complex one, involving mutual recognition of social, but not personal, identity, sexual intent and agreement. Many men in the bar, then, are not engaged in conversation, but are standing along a wall or by themselves at a vantage point in the room so that they may be seen as well as see, and are scanning faces and bodies.

Occasionally, we may see a glance catch and hold another glance. Later, as if in an accidental meeting, the two holders-of-a-glance may be seen in a brief conversation followed by their leaving together. Or, the conversation may be omitted. Casually and unobtrusively, they may arrive at the door at the same time, and leave. If we followed them, we would discover that they were strangers, who by their exchange of glances had agreed to a sexual exchange. The terms of the exchange remaining to be settled will be the place and the nature of the sexual act. A few minutes, or a few hours later, one or both men may reappear in another bar to begin the same procedure all over again, or they may stay together for the night, and the next night seek a new partner. What I have described is one form of "cruising." While the agreements resulting in the one night stand occur in many settings—the bath, the street, the public toilet—and may vary greatly in the elaboration or simplicity of the interaction preceding the culmination in the sexual act, their essential feature is the standardized expectation that sex can be had without obligation or commitment. Irrespective of persons, time, place, and from city to city, in the United States at least, this is a stable, reproducible, standard feature of the interaction.

What stabilizes this pattern of expectation and regularized course of conduct? That is the big question to which I have only partial answers. The promiscuity of the homosexual has been attributed to his psychodynamic structure; among other things, to his primary narcissism. I do not believe that the answer to the question is to be found only in psychodynamic explanations but requires that the system effects of the community be taken into account.

That system, as a sexual market, grows out of the "market mentality." Riesman (1954) comments: "In a market situation pervaded by what Karl Polanyi has termed the 'market mentality' . . . control of the economy will carry with it, to an unusual degree, control of the ethical regime" (p. 60). He suggests that all values are subjected to the market, and are transformed by it; and, further, "it is not the genuine self that is put on the market . . . but the 'cosmetic' self" (pp. 59–60). Nothing is more conspicuous in the gay-bar market than the emphasis on appearance—on dress, manner, and body build. To furnish a genuine self in the exchange of partners, biography and prospects would be essential. In this meeting of strangers, the disengaged character of activities from any ascriptive characteristics is promoted. The pressures toward maintaining secrecy with respect to work and personal biography in homosexual encounters, are derived in part from the functional consequences of their being revealed. The legal, occupational, and personal hazards of identification as a homosexual in our society are amply documented. The risk of information leakage from the gay world to the work world is high.

But if the market mentality pervades society, and if it is the cosmetic self that is put on the market, why should sexual exchange in the relations of male to female be exempt from the characteristics of the one night stand—sex without obligation or commitment? The heterosexual world is *not* exempt, but anything other than monogamous, legally sanctioned, obligated relations is a departure from strongly sanctioned norms, whatever the actual practice may be. That these norms are so strongly sanctioned in the heterosexual world, may be in part a function of the fact that sexuality means more to the female than to the male.[6] Women have more to lose by divesting sexuality of rights, obligations, and commitment because their value in the competitive marriage market partly depends on them as bargaining power, and because their role as child-bearers and child-rearers requires psychological and economic support. The relative absence of women in the homosexual world, the negative sanctions of society against homosexual relationships, the pressures toward secrecy and the risks of revealing one's own personal identity as a homosexual, and the market character of the bar setting in which meetings occur, combine to produce the kind of sexual exchange which we have described as a stable feature of the gay world.

Gay bars also serve other important functions for the community. It is estimated by bartenders that 50 percent of the patrons on any given evening will be habitués who come at least once a week, and frequently, three or four evenings a week. Every bar has its clusters of friends who gather to exchange gossip, to look over the new faces, and to spend a social evening in an atmosphere congenial to them where the protective mask of the day may be dropped. Bars are, therefore, communication centers for the exchange of news and gossip, and for the discussion of problems and hard luck stories. Practical problems such as finding a job, or a place to live, or a lawyer, may be solved with the help of friends or newly met acquaintances. The opening of the newest bar in town, or a place which has recently become "hot," or whether there is a party going on that evening to which one might be invited, are topics of conversation. They are also, paradoxically enough, security operations. While arrests are made in bars, and the presence of vice-squad officers or alcoholic beverage control authorities in plain clothes is an ever-present possibility, the bartender or bar owner will warn the patrons of their presence, if their identity is known—and it frequently is. Warnings will also be passed about particular patrons who are known to be "dirt"; that is, who are likely to rob or demand money or possessions, or to beat up the sexual partner after the consummation of the sexual act. News travels quickly from bar to bar of harassment activities of the authorities.

Bars also serve as induction and training, and integration centers for the community. These functions are difficult to separate. The young man who may have had a few isolated homosexual experiences in adolescence, or indeed none at all, and who is taken to a gay bar by a group of friends whose homosexuality is only vaguely suspected or unknown to him, may find the excitement and opportunities for sexual gratification appealing and thus begin active participation in the community life. Very often the debut, referred to by homosexuals as "coming out," of a person who believes himself to be homosexual but who has struggled against it, will occur in a bar when he, for the first time, identifies himself publicly as a homosexual in the presence of other homosexuals by his appearance in the situation. If he has thought of himself as unique, or has thought of homosexuals as a strange and unusual lot, he may be agreeably astonished to discover large numbers of men who are physically attractive, personable, and "masculine" appearing, so that his hesitancy in identifying himself as a homosexual is greatly reduced. Since he may meet a wide cross section of occupational and socioeconomic levels in the bar, he becomes convinced that far from being a small minority, the gay population is very extensive indeed. Once he has "come out"—that is, identified himself as a homosexual to himself and to some others—the process of education proceeds with rapid pace. Eager and willing tutors—especially if he is young and attractive—teach him the special language, ways of recognizing vice-squad officers, varieties of sexual acts and social types. They also assist him in providing justifications for the homosexual way of life as legitimate, and help to reduce his feeling of guilt by providing him with new norms of sexual behavior in which monogamous fidelity to the sexual partner is rare.

In the bar world the initiate soon acquires a body of knowledge which includes a set of common understandings [7]—what everybody knows. "Everybody knows" that sex can be had without obligation or commitment; it is a meeting of strangers, and the too familiar face may not make out in the sexual market; one can't afford to be seen too frequently or one is counted out of the cruising competition—after the initial newcomer phase; preferences for sexual acts may be specialized and congruence of sexual interests between partners is always problematic; discrepancy between expected sexual behavior and appearance is not a surprise; success in the sexual market will be increased by "masculine" appearance and the appearance of youth; life in the bars for sexual purposes is time limited: older persons (thirty-five or more) may not make out unless they pay for partners; although the potential supply of partners is large, "making out" may be difficult because everyone in the gay world may be afraid of rejection and the criteria of selection may be highly specific.

Earlier I described the homosexual community with the analogy of the iceberg phenomenon, in which the visible part of the community—visible to those who seek it out—is to be found in a round of activities in public institutions, facilities, and areas. I believe, as do homosexuals I have interviewed, that this is a very small part of the total community, and that submerged or hidden, the secret and private activities of the world of social friendship cliques are fundamental to an understanding of the whole. In this world are to be found persons who have established long-term living relationships with another homosexual, and who rarely if ever go to bars or other public establishments because of their sexually predatory and competitive character. They may have had a period of bar-going but now have come to dislike the bar activities or to fear them because of their threat to the stability of an established relationship. Others, especially those of high occupational or socioeconomic status, may restrict their community life to private social cliques because of the fear of exposure or arrest. Others may not enjoy drinking, or may find sufficient sexual and social companionship in homosexual groups, whether they are living alone or in an establishment with another homosexual. There are, of course, many homosexuals who are isolates on the margin of both parts of the community.

The organization of the homosexual world outside of the bars, but linked with it by members common to both, is a loosely knit extended series of overlapping networks of friends. The forms of these networks vary greatly. The three most common are: (1) tightly knit clique structures formed from pairs of homosexually "married" persons, or singles, many of whom are heterosexually married, (2) larger groups with one or more loose clique structures as sociometrically central and a number of peripheral members, and (3) loose networks of friends who may meet only on the occasion of parties. Clique structures and pairs, as well as loose networks of friends, cut across occupational and socioeconomic levels, although those of particular professions or occupations such as teaching, medicine, interior decoration, and dealing in antiques may form association in-groups which have social gatherings. Police exposés of homosexual circles or rings frequently reveal the widespread occupational and age ramifications of such groups. Although the networks are overlapping, the population is so large that nothing occurs like the rapid communication in the criminal underground. For example, in comparing two lists of friends, one of 250 names made by a man of forty and the other of 35 names made by a man of twenty-three, I found only one name common to the two lists although the modal age and range, and the occupations were strikingly similar. The unity of this social world does not consist of close friendship bonds which link person to person throughout the total network, but of common activities, common sexual interests, and a feeling of a common fate which makes them interdependent.

In the cliques, groups, and networks of friends, social occasions such as evening parties, dinners, and cocktail parties are frequent, ranging from the simplest to the most elaborate, and from the most intimate to the large, spur-of-the-moment affairs. "Wedding" anniversaries, birthdays, and other special occasions, much as in the heterosexual world, call for celebrations. Some groups make special efforts to maintain social relations with heterosexual couples, usually ones who are "wise"; that is, are aware of and at least partially accept their homosexuality. These, in my experience, are very rare except in literary, other artistic, or highly sophisticated circles. In the main, members feel uncomfortable in the social presence of heterosexuals, and prefer social occasions in which the guest list is made up of homosexuals so that they can, as their phrase puts it, "let down their hair"; that is, take off their protective masks, use their in-group language, discuss intimate details of their sexual lives, and camp. Although the forms of behavior involved and the definitions of camping given by homosexuals vary widely, we shall not distort too greatly, perhaps, by describing it as usually involving some aspect of the feminine, dramatically displayed in gesture or speech—whether in serious or caricatured form. For example, it is a common practice to use feminine nicknames in homosexual circles, and in the diminutive form. An interchange at a party between two homosexual males in which nicknames are used with effeminate gestures would be a form of what the writer Christopher Isherwood has called "low camp." The social-psychological implications of camping are complex. Some homosexual cliques or groups will not tolerate such behavior, and make every effort to behave in such a way as to minimize any indication of characteristics which would identify them as homosexual.

As contrasted with the one night stand of the gay-bar world, there is constant seeking for more permanent relationships in the social world outside the bars. Indeed, the hope of many who engage in the one-night-stand round of activities is that a particular encounter may lead to a more permanent arrangement. Some long-lasting relationships do begin in the bars but the total system operates against them, as we have seen. In these relationships, sometimes called marriages, complex problems of role management and practical problems of domestic establishments must be solved since they are subject to the strains of a hostile heterosexual society, as well as those of the homosexual world. That many do survive these pressures is well established in my data. Accurate estimates of proportions are impossible since I am not engaged in a survey. In the limited time, I cannot undertake an adequate description of these relationships—of the variety and complexity of their patterns. I want to comment only on one characteristic feature of sex and gender role in relationships in the homosexual world as I have observed them. Contrary to a widespread belief, these are not dichotomized in a clear-cut fashion into masculine and feminine. One does observe pairs with well-defined differentiation but they appear to be in the minority. The terms active or passive partner, masculine or feminine role, as distinguishing members of a pair may be inapplicable to the greater number of these pairs. Instead, the variety and form of the

sexual acts between pair members, the distribution of tasks per-
formed, and the character of their performance do not permit
such a differentiation. New solutions appear for which the old
terms are inapplicable. In part, the emergence of new solutions
may be attributed to the changing culture of the homosexual
world. In what appear to be large sectors of that world, the
stereotype of the effeminate is fought. In some, the result is a
caricature of masculinity. The motorcycle crowd, or the leather
set, with its affectation of the symbols of tough masculinity, is one
form of caricature. In others, the insistence on being men despite
the homosexuality results in a deliberate effort to develop patterns of behavior which are indistinguishable from those of the
heterosexual, except of course in the sexual sphere, and here the
dominant-submissive pattern is consciously resisted.

One of the important features of homosexual subcultures is the
pattern of beliefs, or the justification system. Central to it is the
explanation of why they are homosexuals, and involves the question of choice. The majority of those whom I have interviewed
believe that they were born as homosexuals, or that familial
factors operating very early in their lives determined the outcome.
In any case, it is a fate over which they have no control, and in
which they have no choice. It follows as a consequence that the
possibility of changing to a heterosexual pattern is thought to be
extremely limited. To fight against homosexuality is to fight
against the inevitable since they are fighting against their own
"nature" in its essential form, as they experience it. They believe
that homosexuality is as "natural" for them as heterosexuality is
for others. Such belief patterns are widely shared by those who
identify themselves as members of the community, and who participate in the round of activities we have described. I must
reiterate that not all who engage in homosexual practices have
accepted this identification, and share these beliefs.

In conclusion, I have attempted to describe some features of a
homosexual community in a large urban setting: its ecological
distribution; its visible, public institutions which have been conceptualized as market settings for the exchange of sexual services, and as induction, training, and integration centers for the
community; its visible world of friendship cliques and group
structures in which more stable patterns of relationships are likely
to develop; the common understandings and shared beliefs. In the

time allotted I have not been able to discuss other important features of the community, such as the formal leadership structure, the language patterns, the special humor, the management of impressions by community members in interaction with heterosexual society, and the problems of trust and secrecy within the community. I have tried to show that once an individual enters the community, and begins to enter into its round of activities, he is subject to the beliefs, understandings, and norms of that world. The patterns of behavior which develop, as a consequence, may be as much a function of the system-effects of the community as of need-predispositions which play an important role in shaping the entry routes of some of the members. It is highly probable that it is at least as accurate to speak of the homosexual community as a "deviant community" as to describe it as a "community of deviants."

sex
ethics

CHAPTER 4

Homosexuality: Christian Conviction & Inquiry

ROGER L. SHINN

Contemporary discussion of homosexuality, at least in Western cultures, must move through a desert of accumulated debris before getting at its subject. The debris is constituted of igno-rance, fear, and guilt. The ignorance is partly a lack of accurate information and partly a collection of misinformation propagated in popular culture. The fear is of a threat, real or imagined, to acknowledged values; it is sometimes strongest among people who fear a latent homosexuality in themselves and, in retaliation, lash out against homosexuality in others. The guilt is a long legacy of persecution inflicted upon a minority of society, far out of proportion to the penalties imposed upon people who deviate from customary manners and morals in other ways.

The purpose of this chapter is not to work over the debris, but to get on to the issues posed for Christians by homosexuality as a fact in human life. But we must start by noting the debris in order to avoid confusing it with the subject itself. In particular, we must give some attention to the factor of persecution and the conse-quent guilt of society and church toward its victims.

Dr. Roger L. Shinn is professor of applied Christianity and dean of instruction at Union Theological Seminary, New York City. He was formerly professor of theology at the Divinity School, Vanderbilt University, and chairman of the De-partment of Philosophy at Heidelberg College. Dr. Shinn is the author of *Man: the New Humanism, Tangled World, Moments of Truth, The Existentialist Pos-ture, Christianity and the Problem of History.* He is the coauthor of *We Believe* and the editor of two volumes: *Restless Adventure: Essays on Contemporary Expressions on Existentialism* and *The Search for Identity: Essays on the Ameri-can Character.*

The Victimization of Homosexuals

Whatever our final judgment about homosexuality, there is something peculiarly unhealthy in the zeal of its persecutors. Ours is a culture that, by and large, tolerates much. We are not a people among whom "all hearts are open, all desires known, and from whom no secrets are hid." We permit and encourage considerable anonymity. The common life abounds in material for rumor and innuendo, and gossip is far from rare. Yet a noblesse oblige works to neutralize some insinuations and to protect their victims.

The exception is homosexuality. In high echelons of public life careers have been ruined by episodes of homosexuality. The hint of homosexual behavior is an absolute barrier to numerous public and private jobs. Blackmailers and extortionists fleece their victims with impunity.

An example makes the point. In 1966 the press disclosed the operations of a gang of racketeers who had squeezed millions of dollars out of more than a thousand reputed homosexual victims over roughly a decade. So bold were the operators that in one case two of them, masquerading as New York detectives, entered the Pentagon and led out a high military officer. They managed to mulct him for thousands of dollars before driving him to suicide.[1] One need not have a phobia about the Pentagon to surmise that the private lives of its thousands of denizens offer a good many occasions for possible disclosure and embarrassment. But only on the issue of homosexuality is a moral (or moralistic) passion so built into social institutions as to assure the success of organized blackmail.

Because defense against accusation is so hard and costly, there is no way of knowing how many people suffer severe penalties from their neighbors or from society on this issue. Anybody who writes or speaks publicly against the common cruelty to homosexual persons is likely to receive further evidence by mail—sometimes signed, sometimes anonymous—from victims or their friends and counselors.

The sources of the peculiar horror of homosexuality in our culture are obscure and complex. The Christian tradition, both on the formal and on the popular levels, has had something to do with the case. A very few verses of the Bible, often wrenched out of context and interpreted with doubtful accuracy, have had their influence. Before attributing too much to their power, anybody might ask about many other verses of scripture, more explicit and more emphatic in the original, that have *not* shaped our culture. Churches are showing increasing sensitivity to the harm done by intolerance toward sexual deviance. In Great Britain, after the Wolfenden Report advocated that homosexual relations between consenting adults no longer be considered a crime, the Church of England moved more quickly than Parliament to take up the cause. But the churches are still perplexed and embarrassed by the many issues related to homosexuality.

What I have said thus far presupposes no ethical evaluation of homosexuality itself. It assumes only that, whatever judgment may be made on homosexuality, church and society owe to human beings a concern for justice and a respect for dignity and privacy. Morality is not a valid pretext for cruelty.

Empirical and Theological Factors in Christian Judgment

Any attempt to get at the meaning of homosexuality demonstrates immediately one characteristic of all understanding of human behavior. Understanding comes out of a subtle interaction between two personal-social processes. One is comprised of those moral aesthetic sensitivities about human nature and its possibilities, those purposes and valuations that influence any person's awareness of his world. The other is the acquisition of information empirically available or discoverable by scientific methods of inquiry. Both processes are essential; each is important but by itself is insufficient.

The reason is that meanings, including moral meanings, can never be imposed upon life without regard for the specific facts and circumstances that have meaning for people; hence understanding requires empirical evidence. On the other hand, sheer factual evidence is rarely if ever self-interpreting; it takes on meaning within the experience of persons and communities with their histories, their loyalties, and their purposes.

Human death, to take one of the most obvious of all facts, is never solely a fact; it enters human experience as fate or as accident, as tragedy or absurdity, as defeat or victory, as murder or manslaughter or simple error, as moral outrage or as natural necessity, as enemy or as friend. In any given case the meaning of a death is determined in part by the facts of the situation; it is determined also by the web of experience, beliefs, and commitments by which persons meet the death of themselves and of others.

Christian ethics is not unusual in bringing to any situation a constellation of experiences that contribute to the meanings that can be found in the situation. All ethical thinking does that. The distinctive quality of Christian ethics is that the experiences, the memories, and the expectations that it brings to all phenomena are related to the experience of Jesus Christ. It does not expect any collection of unevaluated facts to add up to significant human meaning; it finds meaning as the awareness of Christ alerts persons to the possibilities and perils of life. Hence there are theological factors at work in any Christian apprehension of empirical situations.

Christian judgments on human conduct are subject to change. The hastiest glance at history will show such change in judgments of behavior—whether sexual, economic, military, racial, political, or almost anything else. The Christian community, living in history, modifies its judgments—both for better and for worse —in the light of new experiences, new temptations, new insights. But it always—insofar as it is true to its faith—brings to experience the awareness of Christ and of the biblical history that tells it of Christ.

All this means that Christian ethics approaches a problematic situation within a context of inquiry that in some important way is given. There is a discipline of Christian inquiry. The Christian community does not ask simply how men may have most fun or use up most consumer goods or lead the most untroubled lives. It does not even ask how they may achieve the fullest self-expression or happiness. It is concerned for the good of man, not for abstract causes. But in searching for the good of man it sees a cruciform pattern in life. "If any man would come after me, let him deny himself and take up his cross and follow me. For whoever would save his life will lose it, and whoever loses his life for my sake will find it" (Matt. 16:24–25).

Thus a paradox is built into the heart of Christian ethics. The paradox has been misused. Christians have prescribed crosses for others while exalting themselves. They have deceived themselves by cultivating trivial forms of self-denial while indulging in frantic self-aggrandizement. They have elaborated heresies that denied the joyful recognition of the good of life, forgetting that their Lord came that men might "have life, and have it abundantly" (John 10:10). But the recognition of a cruciform quality in life, despite its history of distortions, is inherent in Christian ethics. It distinguishes the Christian ethic from the most prevalent alternative in Western culture, the ethic of self-realization that extends from Aristotle to contemporary philosophy.

This ineradicably theological factor in Christian ethics does not of itself provide many precise ethical judgments. Certainly it does not prescribe a code of behavior for contemporary man. If anybody thinks that it does, he might try to answer the simple question "Where?" He can hardly locate the authoritative code in the teachings of Augustine, Thomas Aquinas, or Calvin. If he proposes the Bible, again the question is "Where?" Does any contemporary person take the book of Leviticus as an adequate guide for the ethical perplexities of contemporary urban life? Or, to use a more embarrassing example, does anyone so take the Sermon on the Mount? Certainly there is no automatic process by which a believer can lift out of biblical or historical tradition a moral commandment to meet a contemporary perplexity.

The theological component in Christian decision-making is a context of inquiry and a sensitivity of perception. It is a possibility of self-understanding and the understanding of others. It is an awareness of divine gifts and divine demands. It is a set of convictions, in some ways unassailable and in other ways not fully defined, about the good of man, about what is wrong with him, and about new possibilities for human life.

Among the Christian convictions about man are an awareness of the gift of freedom and unique personhood in each individual, a sensitivity to the needs and opportunities of life in community, an awareness of the sin that infects human life, and an openness to the possibilities of personal transformation. These convictions, although not codified, are not utterly vague. They have quite concrete meaning, even though the meaning cannot be readily prescribed.

A comparison with two other styles of ethics is possible. The ethic of self-realization, which I have already mentioned, says to the person: "Be yourself. Realize your possibilities." Against it stand the many ethics of imposed standards, which say: "Be the self that some authority (the church, the police force, the peer group, your parents, the popular culture) tells you to be." The Christian ethic differs from the first alternative because man, as he is, is not a good enough model for himself. It differs from the second because it (the second) asks the person to conform to the expectations of others. In contrast to both, the Christian ethic says: "Become the person that only you, in your created freedom and by God's grace, can become."

The theological factor, as I have described it, is experiential; but it belongs to the type of human experience associated with man's moral imagination, his human sensitivity, and his religious faith. In understanding the concrete decisions of life it must be joined with the kind of information that comes from empirical investigation of facts, both in the manner of practical everyday observation and in the manner of scientific investigation. Especially in the understanding of a topic like homosexuality, which has often been obscured by superstition and erroneous information, clarification of the facts can contribute to understanding of their meaning.

Thus the knowledge that men (and equally women, for that matter) are not divided into two opposite classifications, homosexual and heterosexual, but can be placed on a heterosexual-homosexual continuum, is significant for the understanding of human responses and behavior.[2] The information does not, of itself, dictate what behavior is to be encouraged or discouraged. But it enables persons to understand better themselves and their own approval or condemnation of others.

Similarly, information about the causes of homosexuality has some significance for an understanding of its human meaning. If, as some psychiatrists maintain, homosexuality is a matter of arrested psychosexual development, that bit of knowledge says something about its desirability. If, on the other hand, it is a frequent characteristic of persons who in every ascertainable respect are mature and healthy, that says something else about it. Presumably some progress in the resolution of such arguments is possible. In neither case does the evidence establish an incontrovertible ethical judgment—and in neither case could the evidence possibly justify the persecution of homosexuals that I have already criticized. But further information is likely to influence normative judgments.

Another question, subject to empirical inquiry, is the changeability of sexual responses, both emotional and behavioral. To the extent that a person is free to change himself and his personal characteristics, new possibilities are available to him. To the extent that he cannot change, he must learn to live with himself as he is. Again no ethical conclusion is dictated; the changeability of a person's character does not itself establish that he should change, nor does the unchangeability of it in some respects mean that it is in those respects admirable. But possibilities of change are evidence of freedom; and what a man does with his freedom, as contrasted with conditions he cannot change, is always an ethical issue.

Yet the subtlety of this issue forbids hasty conclusions. Suppose a man changes his sexual behavior by turning himself into a manipulated object. There are methods of treatment that, in some cases, can do just that. If a man is homosexually responsive and heterosexually unresponsive, behavioristic techniques of "therapy" may change him, by subjecting him to homosexual stimuli accompanied by pain (e.g., electric shock), then to heterosexual stimuli accompanied by pleasurable experiences. Thus he may be conditioned or directed toward heterosexuality. The troubling question is whether such treatment does not succeed in bringing the person to conformity with the dominant moral culture, while violating his own freedom and selfhood.

In one other area—the relation of homosexuality to other personal and cultural patterns—increasing knowledge can be illuminating. If, as appears to be the case in current experience, homosexual relationships are in general less stable and less genuinely interpersonal than heterosexual relationships, why is this so? Is homosexuality inherently instable, or do cultural patterns make it so? If homosexuals frequently live in a subculture with undesirable characteristics, is it homosexuality or is it the prejudice of the society that produces such a culture? What is cause and what is effect? Normal marriage, although vulnerable enough, is supported by many legal, moral, and economic institutions of society. Homosexual relations, without such support, are likely to find transitory, sub-rosa expression. Information about the stability and truly personal quality of homosexual relations is incomplete. But enough knowledge is available to dispel some popular prejudices.

In all of these cases accurate information about homosexuality has some implications for understanding its meaning. The inadequacy of present knowledge is one reason why many judgments about homosexuality must be tentative. Even so, it remains the case that information alone does not establish meaning or dictate valuation. At the present time the conflicts over the meaning of homosexuality are as great among the scientists who have done research on the subject as among laymen. Such specialists as Albert Ellis, Daniel Cappon, Edmund Bergler, and Irving Bieber give the impression that homosexuality is a neurotic phenomenon, subject to correction by therapy; whereas Clara Thompson, Judd Marmor, Evelyn Hooker, and Wardell Pomeroy find data leading to friendlier judgments. Although most of these scholars are psychiatrically trained, they probably could not tell for themselves with any certainty to what extent their findings arise from hostility or friendliness to homosexual persons.

The Traditional Christian Normative Judgment

The Christian tradition over the centuries has affirmed the heterosexual, monogamous, faithful marital union as normative for the divinely given meaning of the intimate sexual relationship. Alongside this, it has recognized a valid vocation of celibacy for some persons.

Within this tradition Christians have sometimes contributed to, sometimes tried to correct, the peculiarly harsh judgments against homosexuality that have been prominent in our culture. Today there are determined efforts within the church to make amends for the severe judgmentalism and the isolation that the church often has inflicted, and frequently persists in inflicting, upon homosexual persons.

There is widespread Christian recognition today of the need for increased understanding that may lead to the revision of many traditional attitudes. But for the most part the renunciation of the ethic of condemnation has not led to an ethic of endorsement. Daniel Day Williams has summarized well, without necessarily stating as his own, a characteristic position in theological ethics today: "Homosexuality—whatever its genetic, cultural, and psychological aspects—involves modes of human experience which are in some way deviant from the fullest possibilities of sexual life which are realized only in heterosexual relationships." [3]

Certainly there are impressive biblical foundations for such a position. The Bible, I have already insisted, does not deliver to the Christian a code of conduct for modern life. Hence there is something futile about the enterprise, occasionally pursued, of tracking down all the biblical texts referring to homosexuality and arguing from them to a set of norms for today. The battle of proof-texts goes on, but not to much avail. What the Bible communicates to the Christian is a revelation of divine love and the possibilities of responsive human love, including the meaning and possibilities of human sexuality. In that sense, rather than in any amassing of miscellaneous texts from a variety of historical contexts, there is a clear endorsement of heterosexuality.

It is most evident in Jesus' teaching on the fundamental meaning of sexuality, in which he quotes and makes his own certain statements from the first two chapters of Genesis: "But from the beginning of creation, 'God made them male and female.' 'For this reason a man shall leave his father and mother and be joined to his wife, and the two shall become one' " (Mark 10:6–8).

Christians have had long practice in misusing the words of Jesus. It is a misuse if a church, which has long tolerated deviations from almost all the teachings of Jesus, uses such a text to condemn those who deviate from it. It is a misuse if Christians violate the integrity of other men and women by imposing upon them the understanding of sex that most Christians derive from Christ, the Christian tradition, and their own experience. But it is not a misuse for Christians to testify that their faith has made them aware of the peculiar meaning of the one-flesh relationship between male and female under God.

Christians have usually believed that the ethical awareness given to them through Christ, although not necessarily demonstrable outside the community of faith, meets some similar intimations or signs of confirmation in wider human experience. They believe that the *Logos* made flesh in Christ is the same *Logos* through which the world was made. They do not expect the Christian faith and insight to be confirmed by unanimous agreement of all people, even all decent and idealistic people. But they do expect the fundamental Christian motifs to have some persuasiveness in general experience.

Such a persuasiveness is evident in the reasoning of Erich Fromm. (Fromm will not be offended to be identified as a non-Christian, since he would feel unjustly treated if we called him a Christian.)

The male-female polarity is also the basis for interpersonal creativity. This is obvious biologically in the fact that the union of sperm and ovum is the basis for the birth of a child. But in the purely psychic realm it is not different; in the love between man and woman, each of them is reborn.[4]

It is important to examine exactly the reasoning involved here. The point is not to invoke the authority of Fromm (since other authorities take other positions), but to examine what he is saying. His argument is *not* that the purpose of heterosexual love is procreation—or that procreation is somehow necessary to justify sexual love. He is rather pointing to an analogy between biological and psychic creativity, an analogy that, as he goes on to say, is impossible in homosexuality. He also goes on to say that many heterosexual relations fail in this love. There is no ground here for the equation of heterosexual with good and homosexual with bad, but there is a clear affirmation of the meaning possible in authentic love between one man and one woman, and impossible otherwise.[5]

If there is in Christian theology a clear emphasis on the normative place of heterosexual love, there is an equally clear awareness that no legalism is adequate to define authentic sexuality and sexual love. Although the Christian tradition endorses the monogamous, faithful, heterosexual marital union, such a marriage may still be joyless or exploitative.

Certainly there have been polygamous families with more love and mutual concern than many monogamous families. There have been promiscuous and adulterous liaisons with more personal concern than some technically faithful unions. There have been homosexual relationships with more mutual appreciation than some heterosexual marriages. Any legalistic definition of conditions that make sex "right" is a trap. Even so, it is still possible to maintain that there is a normative expression of sexual love, as Christian faith understands the meaning of such love.

To many honest representatives of homophile groups, this position will seem entirely inadequate. It will not help to add that there is no insinuation here that any given homosexual individual is morally inferior to any given heterosexual individual or to heterosexual people as a class. Nor will it be enough to continue that, in Christian terms, no person ever achieves righteousness or moral excellence, but the best of men are sinful and live by the mercy of

God. All such talk, in the face of the history of moral condemnation of homosexuals, is likely to appear as pious prattle concealing an unbearable condescension.

In reply, all that can be said is that some Christians genuinely believe the position that has been set forth here and that they believe the consistent theme of Christian ethics requires the maintenance of moral apprehensions derived from Christ, together with a refusal to use those apprehensions to condemn those whom Christ did not condemn.

The Current Theological Discussion

The position I have sketched here is not a final verdict. In contemporary theological discussions there are at least three other distinguishable possibilities that deserve discussion.

One of these is the decisive reaffirmation of the biblical tradition as stated by Karl Barth. The central theme in all Barth's theology and ethics is the overwhelming grace of God. The ethic is thoroughly biblical. Barth is not interested in the many empirical questions I have raised in this discussion, and his ethic is far less tentative in its moral judgment than the position I have described above in the language of Daniel Day Williams. Barth believes that man's sexuality is inherent in his created nature and destiny, that men and women both know themselves only in relation to the other sex, that homosexuality is a rejection of creatureliness and an idolatry. It is a malady of "perversion, decadence, and decay." Thus far the judgment seems harsh. Yet Barth is not interested in moral condemnation. Christ has conquered sin, and Barth perceives men as elected to redemption in Christ. So his message to every person, however perplexed or troubled by life's problems, is the message of exuberant confidence in God's love. The implication is that no one should try to defend or justify homosexuality; equally no one should condemn any person or despair over any sin.[6]

A second possibility appears in the thought of Helmut Thielicke, who is more interested in the empirical study of homosexuality than Barth, but no less concerned with its theological meaning. Thielicke plainly regards homosexuality as an abnormality, a distortion or depravation of the normal created order. But in a world where all men share in fallen and distorted existence, "there is not the slightest excuse for maligning the constitutional homosexual morally or theologically." When the homosexual can change to heterosexuality, he should seek treatment or healing. Where he cannot, he may find it possible to sublimate his homosexual desires. If not, he may seek "to structure the man-man relationship in an *ethically responsible* way." Such an effort is hazardous, given the patterns of society; and Thielicke does not want to change those patterns basically, except that he endorses the Wolfenden proposals for removing the criminal status of adult homosexual behavior and he opposes the judgmentalism of society. He would encourage the homosexual to make the best of his painful situation without pretending that it is normal.[7]

The third possibility is a full acceptance of homosexuality. The theme is stated in the well-known statement of the English Quakers: "One should no more deplore 'homosexuality' than left-handedness. . . . Homosexual affection can be as selfless as heterosexual affection, and therefore we cannot see that it is in some way morally worse."[8] A similar position has been stated persuasively by some Christian pastors who have worked closely with homosexuals and homophile organizations.[9] Some have recommended that the church acknowledge homosexuality to the extent of providing a rite of homosexual marriage. This latter position marks un abrupt departure from theological and liturgical tradition, but it stems from a genuine concern for persons.

Christian ethics rarely prescribes final forms and institutions for human behavior. More specifically, this is not the time in history for final judgment on the meaning and ethical import of homosexuality. Information about the phenomena, the causes, and the possibilities of change is still inadequate. Meanwhile the three themes just described all have a justifiable place within the conversations of the Christian community as it seeks further wisdom on a troubling issue.

As Christians seek better understanding on this issue, they have a responsibility to remain open to any new sources of information and insight. They have a similar responsibility to remain faithful to the moral apprehensions of the Christian gospel. Among those apprehensions those that have been most neglected in the past practice of the church in this sphere are the sensitivities that warn against condemnation and that evoke compassion.

CHAPTER 5

The Paradox of Man & Woman

RALPH W. WELTGE

Men and women are different. That is hardly news. Yet one thing homosexuals, heterosexuals, Christians, secularists, and behavioral scientists all agree on is the congenital difference between the human male and female. Only fools would dispute it, and only trans-sexuals would try to change it.

Freud's remark that "anatomy is destiny" merits some skepticism. While anatomy settles some issues like gender identification and the designation of who bears children, it confounds an issue like homosexuality. For sexuality is more than anatomy and its functions. Society defines and assigns social-sexual roles to each gender, and expands the meaning of sexual identification in the process of ordering it. To be a man, then, means more than being a male.

Human sexuality is unique in being largely liberated from the control of instinct. Among all the species man alone has real sexual freedom and is therefore morally responsible for his sexuality. Living east of Eden and forbidden an innocent and unconscious immersion in creatureliness, only man asks the question of identity. His human identity is an open question because that identity is not finished by nature or completely bound to it.

Sexual identification is an integral factor of human identification. Anatomy is given, but the meaning and ordering of sexuality

---

The Rev. Ralph W. Weltge is a staff member of the United Church Board for Homeland Ministries, and specializes in the church's ministry to the new generation. At present he is on loan to Urban Young Adult Action, Inc., an ecumenical agency which works with the new generation around social and political issues on the urban scene. Mr. Weltge was formerly on the staff of the youth department of the World Council of Churches in Geneva, Switzerland. He is the author of The Church Swept Out.

is a human creation. And the irreducible biological base, male and female, can support a bewildering variety of sex-role configurations as the cross-cultural studies show. Human sexuality is plastic and polymorphic in its nascent state. This indeterminacy, which reflects man's transcendence and freedom, makes sexual identification both possible and necessary. To be born a male may be destiny, but to be a man is a human decision and a social construction.

The Norm in Biblical Faith

A Christian deals with ethical issues in a context which includes scripture, and the issue of homosexuality is no exception. Biblical material exists which speaks per se to the issue or has been traditionally interpreted as referring to it. In the Christian community the discussion often starts there. Actually the references in that material are least helpful, and used in isolation will miss the crux of the issue.[1]

One must turn to a broader theme for biblical reference because the issue of homosexuality is one part of a larger theological problem; i.e., the enigmatic relationship between man and woman. The identity of man and of woman in the paradox of similarity and difference sets the terms of reference and becomes the previous question.

The sexual norm honored by church tradition has its origin in Old Testament references subsequently ratified by Jesus. In terms of literature the creation stories are prehistoric sagas, and they include a basic affirmation of the mystery of man and woman. One could summarize the theme this way: God created man as male and female, and "it was very good." Sexuality is a good gift to be gladly received and duly celebrated. For "it is not good that . . . man should be alone." God intended man to be fully human within this primordial distinction. Man and woman are created for each other, to be one flesh. But they do not exist for each other alone; together they are created for others and for God. Therefore, their existence as one flesh is a prototype of man's love for his fellowman, and a human parable of God's love for all men.[2]

The creation stories are not descriptive facts, not science or an explanation of nature and its origins. The Bible does not begin with creation but with exodus. These stories are "flashbacks" originating after the exodus from slavery, after the identity of Israel was first formed by the liberation event. As C. A. van Peursen has noted, "Man acquires his identity by the stories he tells about God." [3]

No new facts are given because man has always known about the male-female arrangement. The stories represent Israel positing the meaning of sexual identification in God, in the same liberating power who meets his people in the events of their history. Faith transforms old facts with the proclamation that sexual distinction is normative for man. The daily refrain of creation is "it was good." Man also acquires his sexual identity by the stories he tells about God. For on the basis of that narrated norm the family and society will teach and model out the defined sexual roles.

Interpreting the Norm

In succinct form the biblical norm for human sexuality is this: man and woman joined together as one flesh in faithful love. One persuasive interpretation of it has been given by Karl Barth. He derives ethical insights from theological formulations, in this case the Christian confession about creation.

Barth's basic thesis is that man is never solitary because being human means existence in relationship to others, those others being God and men. To be a man is to be a fellowman. And in human life this fellow-humanity is revealed in the relationship of man to woman. Man's first and fundamental fellowman is woman.

Barth begins with the created fact of sexual differentiation. Sexuality means difference, distinction, and discontinuity. This created otherness is good and can neither be avoided nor overcome. To be concretely human means to be a man *or* a woman because there is no neutral or abstract sexuality.

This fact excludes two variations of sexual indentification. One is switching sex roles which leads to an erosion of the distinction. While masculine and feminine traits are relative, and cultural roles do change, the important thing is maintaining distinction. The second variation is the attempt to get beyond one's own and the opposite sex to a "third sex," or higher mode of being. This is the search for an existence which is purely human, abstractly human, sexless. It is a mythological escape into an identity that is neither male nor female, or both at once. Reality means a person is he or she, but never a neutral "it."

That is half the story. The obverse of sexual distinction is the continuity or covenant between man and woman. Barth says there is no such thing as an isolated and self-sufficient male or female life. "Neither is the man without the woman, neither the woman without the man, in the Lord" (1 Cor. 11:11, KJV). Being a fellowman means relationship and interdependence as well. Man's first fellowman is woman, both in distinction and relationship.

> We have to say both that man is necessarily and totally man *or* woman, and that as such and in consequence he is equally and totally man *and* woman. He cannot wish to liberate himself from the differentiation and exist beyond his sexual determination as mere man . . . nor can he wish to liberate himself from the relationship and be man without woman or woman apart from man.[4]

If "it is not good that . . . man should be alone," we are advised to oppose all forms of sex seclusion which are more than incidental and provisional deprivations; that is, separations on principle. That would set the church against religious communities, the celibate priesthood, prisons, the homosexual community, and the military service. "Who commands or permits them to run away from each other?"[5]

The continuity of this covenant between man and woman Barth calls "the prototype of all I and thou, of all individuality in which man and man differ from and yet belong to each other."[6] The norm for sexuality thus points beyond itself to the ultimate Christian norm, which is love. It is a model for achieving co-humanity and community in spite of differences such as race, class, education, or culture. This orientation to the other is an openness to the opposite, in this case to the one who identifies me sexually by his or her otherness. It is the relationship to woman that makes a man a man, and vice versa.

It is prudent to take the partnership seriously also in theology and listen to a woman theologian! In her book *Man and Woman: Similarity and Difference,* Francine Dumas deals primarily with the changing roles of women in society. That issue is part of this theological theme and she reaches a similar conclusion.

> To be human is first of all to recognize my fellow in the other and then in my fellow, the other. The church, the body of Christ, is the place of this double gesture. Man and woman live this out whenever their encounter is genuine. They are similar . . . and it is in this similarity that their difference is revealed.[7]

Dumas takes up the cause of that majority which has suffered discrimination on the basis of sex since time began. Woman is the original sexual outcast from the male world, there surrounded by fears, myths, demons, and taboos. The paradox of man and woman has been repeatedly broken by man, usually on the side of separation. "Let us add . . . that it is the separation of the sexes that creates uniformity, and their similarity and their life in common in all fields of existence which diversifies."[8] It is not the merger of the sexes but their separation which produces androgynous sexuality.

The Ethical Bind

Barth rejects the homosexual orientation and relates it to idolatry, as does Paul in Romans 1:25–27. Homosexuality denies God's purpose in creation by excluding the other sex and attempting to be human alone, without the primary fellowman. Substituting a man for woman is maleness curved in upon itself—a sovereign maleness which lives in self-satisfaction and self-sufficiency. The other partner in co-humanity, who was also created in God's image, is exchanged for an image of the self. Homosexuality is sin in the form of male self-deification.

The case Barth makes against homosexuality is impressive. Other than a degree of "theological overkill," its weakness lies in categorically condemning homosexuality as if the phenomena were uniform behavior, the causes of it known, and the choice a simple moral perversion. This exposes the vulnerability of Barth's own methodology. Working deductively to derive ethical decisions from dogmatic formulations, he underplays the existential context and takes little counsel from the other human disciplines.

At this point in the discussion I feel a bind after having read some of the literature and listened to homosexuals themselves. One's sympathies become divided, as is often the case when commuting between the church and some subculture alien to it. A position in between gives new perspectives on both the church and the homophile world. Each deserves some critique as well as a measure of support.

Specifically, the bind I feel is not located in the Christian norm itself. Theologically I subscribe to that norm with conviction. For me the problem lies in how the norm is used in church and society, what is done by design or default to those who violate it. The homosexual bears pressures, indignities, and injustices which demand relief. The question is how to take up his cause without either sacrificing the norm or sanctioning its use as a cover for persecution. For persecuting homosexuals violates other norms also honored by a Christian ethic.

A Critique of Church Practice

The only institution which treats the homosexual worse than the church is the military service. Both have homosexuals within their ranks. Exposure in one case will mean court marital and a dishonorable discharge; and the other involves silent shunning if your status is lay, and an urgent call to serve God elsewhere if you are clergy. In each case the homosexual is drummed out of the community because regulations have been violated.

Admittedly, homosexual survival is more likely among the Christians because there love and grace do have constitutional status. And an institution where the sexes live out the encounter of otherness is more secure in the face of deviation than one which is homosexual (i.e., the same sex) by choice and ethos. Sexual segregation fears most what it helps induce, and requires the strongest negative sanctions to maintain itself. So the church is more free than the military while still being a long way off from true Christian liberality.

The bind becomes tight when one realizes that supporting the norm entails allies he does not care to have. Ghosts of the Christian past are summoned forth to tell the sad history of the homosexual in the hands of the church as it moved from a policy of extermination to quarantine and persecution. Today the heirs of an anti-sexualism which fears the power of sex far more than it celebrates its goodness have an odd preoccupation with the sins of sex and count them the more serious violations of the law. Racism, poverty, and war, which derive from social injustices that destroy countless people, cannot muster the same revulsion and moral outrage that greets a couple of morals charges and a rumor of rising fornication. With priorities like that the straight church is the real moral deviant.

No doubt the church is guilty of bad faith on this issue. Bad faith is earnestly believing that you have no choice, no alternatives, that you must think and act in certain ways because duty demands it. In this case it means believing that religion requires the church representative to condemn and ostracize the homosexual, treating him as a moral leper. The Torquemada type can even quote scripture to justify the persecution of sexual heretics.

What is served by this, of course, is not the Lord but the self-righteousness of the persecutors. The godly never feel so holy as when they are excoriating sexual sinners. People often legitimate themselves by hating a despised group set up as a counter-image. If your religious identity is unsure then secure it by condemning sinners. If your sexual identity is shaky then shore it up by despising homosexuals. Or, as Peter Berger has put it: "One beats the Negro to feel white. One spits on homosexuals to feel virile." [9]

In this process the identity of the persecutor is legitimized by the negative identity of the persecuted. The homosexual is a perfect fall guy because his suffering provides a double reward— it makes one both a "man" and a "Christian." But any identity established that way is an idol because it requires human sacrifices as the substance of its cultic practice. Church persecution of the homosexual is idolatry achieved in the very call of duty.

Bad faith is always a flight from freedom, in this case the freedom of the gospel itself. What the Christian faith *does* require is that the church live by the same grace it proclaims in Jesus Christ. In other words, one has to use Barth against Barth and say that even though homosexuality violates the norm for sexuality, that same violation is also overcome by the triumph of grace. Grace includes the homosexual. Grace is the first and last word of liberation which the church has to say to him. Therefore the spirit of condemnation is as much unfaith as it is bad faith.

The critique of the church supports the homosexual's cause where it accuses the church of providing religious legitimation for social injustices. By mandate the church must honor the humanity of men, including those who do not honor the church's sexual norms. The homosexual has every right to expect the church to serve as an *advocatus humanum,* to be his protagonist in obtaining full civil liberties, law reforms, and the end of sexual bigotry. For the church's advocacy role is part of its own identity, in no way contingent on the presence or absence of virtue in those whose cause it takes up.

A Critique of the Homosexual Ideology

Just as one violates the humanity of the homosexual by equating him totally with that identity, so also the homosexual violates his own humanity when his sexuality becomes the ruling authority of his self-image. In the giving and receiving of names, identifications are made and images are created. In Hebrew thought a name not only distinguishes a person but also reveals the nature of its bearer. A name is a claim. It proclaims the identity and destiny of a person or a place. The game of identifications is serious play because real men can be destroyed and imposters created.

One demonic dimension of this issue is the virulent mythos in American culture which dichotomizes male sexual identity. Male stereotypes abound, and one is either a "man's man" or no man. The young man is given an either/or choice, which is a male burlesque of the man/woman paradox. People with incidental homosexual experience are quickly labeled "homosexuals," which they are not. The mutually exclusive categories present a choice between mutually inauthentic identities. The male dichotomy violates the paradox of man and woman by turning difference into dualism, and ignoring the similarity of the sexes, like the traits they share in common or the "feminine characteristics" also incorporated by men.

We see ourselves through the eyes of others and become what people call us. Giving someone a negative identity like "homosexual" prepares him for a destiny of dehumanization. A whole person is reduced to a negative abstraction of sexuality because men are more easily murdered if their full humanity is ignored. Yet the recipient usually aids the conspiracy by accepting the negative name and merely trying to make it a positive identity. Thus the major counteroffensive of homosexuals is the protestation that "gay is good," that gay is a sexual style of life every bit as moral and meaningful as heterosexuality.

But there is no such thing as "the homosexual" in reality. There are only human beings with more or less sexual experience with the same and/or the opposite sex. The name homosexual is a mythical identity which some impose to dishonor others, and others accept to honor themselves. In either case the name is a metonym for a real man whose identity transcends his sex history. Being itself bogus, the name can no more authenticate the homosexuality of the man who proudly claims it than it can prove the heterosexuality of the man who uses it as an epithet. In short, if no one is humanized by spitting on the man who spits on woman, neither does glorifying that identity serve to humanize the man who treats woman as a "sexual nigger." The man who claims the name homosexual as the parameter of his identity constructs the gay version of an old idolatry—building your life around an erection.

There is an analogous form of bad faith in the self-image of the homosexual and the ideology which justifies his identity. Again, bad faith is a flight from freedom and a hiding behind the excuses of nature and necessity.

On the one hand homosexuals disclaim all moral responsibility for their orientation and acts because no choice was involved. ("Did you choose to be a heterosexual?" "No." "Well, neither did I choose to be a homosexual. But I am one. I cannot help it and I cannot change it.") Since choice is a precondition of morality this kind of blind determinism serves as a convenient moral alibi. The homosexual cannot be held responsible if his orientation is fate and his sexual practices are a compulsion. Therefore he believes in a kind of "sexual double predestination," and God, or society, or parents become responsible in his stead. Freedom is abandoned for the easy innocence of powerlessness.

On the other hand the homosexual claims this is responsible sexuality. The homosexual ideology seeks to justify the orientation as morally good, statistically normal, biologically natural, aesthetically beautiful, and—sometimes—theologically sound. The point is that the avowed determinism which creates homosexuals is transformed into a "blessed determinism." That is saying more than that the best should be made out of the inevitable. It contends that the creation of homosexuals is positively good, a preferred condition for at least those who participate in it. What was not chosen happens to be also a very good choice made by somebody. It is also a way to keep your virginity in the very process of losing it.

The self-deceptions become rather noticeable when the ideology transmogrifies the homosexual into a veritable saint and claims fellatio as a sexual sacrament. What reason is there to believe that homosexuals are necessarily more honest about themselves, or less prone to self-justification, than other men? I am convinced that the homosexual is justified, but justified by God's grace and not by homosexuality. That grace is an absolutely free gift, given without precondition, reservation, or judgment. Grace requires only one thing, a decision of faith. It allows no complacency, no neutrality, and no excuses. When a man meets grace he is called into its service. His life is transformed by it and he lives in gratitude for it. Grace gives him a fully human identity.

There are some things the homophile community cannot expect from the church. One is the abandonment of the norm honoring the goodness of creation in the paradox of man and woman. That is the church's strongest point both in terms of theology and in what the overwhelming majority of people seem to be doing sexually. Few men want to alter such a rare and happy coincidence between God's intention and their own! Substituting another norm derived from the behavioral sciences or the homosexual ideology is not likely. Realism and strategy suggest that achieving a suspended judgment or even apathy from the church is a more sensible goal for the homophile movement.

As a corollary, the church is not about to sacralize homosexuality. That would mean going beyond neutrality to wholehearted support. Even during its present state of insanity, theology probably could not manage the contortions of thought and reinterpretation of scripture that bringing it off would require. (After all, what could be harder to sell the church than the amazing discovery of scholars that Eve was actually a man in drag?) In terms of symbolics, sacralization would require a homosexual marriage liturgy which no church commission on worship is in the process of preparing. All the church can offer is a continuation of the present arrangement of "living in sin without benefit of clergy."

Penultimate Love

I have taken one route out of the bind caused by the apparent valence between the Christian norm and the unjust treatment of homosexuals. It has meant supporting the norm while at the same time advocating the human dignity and rights of those violating it.

Thus I have argued that there is no causal relationship between the norm and the injustices by theological necessity. Grace has intervened and broken the valence. The Christian views men "with Christ in between"; that is, under the power and authority of his grace. Consequently, supporting the norm does not demand the persecution of homosexuals, and breaking idols does not require slaying their priests. That happens only because of the bad faith and lack of grace in those who justify inhumanities in the name of God. God will have no part of it.

There is another way out of the bind. Instead of attacking the injustices which homosexuals suffer one may attack the norm itself. This answer believes that the best way to obtain relief is to sacrifice the norm and substitute one which will give homosexuality equal moral status. For norms are often easier to change than people's behavior.

For example, it is possible to adopt an alternate normative framework like one of the behavioral sciences. The human sciences do furnish homosexuals with a good deal of support. Homosexual behavior is natural and normal within the theoretical contexts of those disciplines. The growing body of data produced by sex research can be made authoritative because it reveals what people actually do. Incidence is taken as an index and made normative, standardizing the sexual status quo. Only that is not the way Christians normally arrive at norms.

Yet, one need not abandon theology in order to change the traditional norm. With good theological and biblical support it may be done by substituting the ultimate Christian norm of love in pure and simple form. What happens is best shown in a three-step process.

1. The traditional Christian norm is *man and woman joined as one flesh in faithful love.* By affirming the paradox of man and woman it excludes homosexuality. Man and woman means husband and wife, since marriage is the analogue in social structures. The norm points to love, but love fulfilling the paradox of sexual identification, not dissolving it.

2. The initial shift restates the norm this way: *a loving relationship between man and woman.* Love becomes the first and modal term. The paradox of man and woman is honored but not the regulatory agency of marriage. Homosexuality is still excluded.

3. The last step in this reduction process puts it this way: *a*

loving relationship between two people. The homosexual liaison becomes moral because the norm has been reduced simply to the love requirement. Love is not just the modal term but the *only* term. The paradox of man and woman has been dissolved in "people," a reference which is androgynous. This position concludes: "Whether any form of sex (hetero, homo, or auto) is good or evil depends on whether love is fully served." [10]

Sex and love are not coterminous. In fact, as Mort Sahl has observed, "The biggest innovation that could happen to sex is love." [11] Love is possible without sex, as sex is possible without love. /Being the ultimate term, love gives meaning to sex and sex lives in the service of love./ This love is definitively revealed in Jesus Christ who is himself the identification of life's final meaning. What he is, love is. All things are subject to him, including human sexuality.

The norm of love is the final goal and the final judgment on all life. Rejoice whenever love becomes an event in human relationships for there the ultimate has entered human history.\However, Bonhoeffer reminds us that the ultimate functions not to destroy the penultimate, but to fulfill it. Sexual identification is penultimate and stands under the ultimate norm. Yet the norm of love does not destroy sexuality by dissolving the paradox of man and woman. It does not transport us into heaven where angels are men, and women are not given in marriage. Love does not create asexuality, much less anti-sexuality, but a fully human sex life.

God alone lives beyond sexuality. Love lives in history where sexual identification is ineradicable. And love fulfills that paradox by directing man sexually to his fellowman, woman. It also directs man to his fellowman, whether man or woman, in a style of life which is fully human because it participates in love which is the ultimate meaning of life. To be a man, fully human, is to be a man to woman and a man to man.

Shall the church say "Yes" or "No" to homosexuality? Well, neither, in the last analysis. That is not equivocation about the issue but only faithfulness to the church's task among men. The church is not required to pronounce God's no on the homosexual and abandon him in condemnation. Neither is it supposed to justify him with some improved and better human yes. All the church finally has to say is God's yes to man, which is his sovereign grace, his final word to every man. "Mercy triumphs over judgment" (James 2:13). That is the first and last word.

CHAPTER 6

A Brief for a New Homosexual Ethic

NEALE A. SECOR

This chapter is a critique of the liberal Protestant ethic which concludes that Christians should "accept" the homosexual as another sinner. It is an argument against too easily agreeing with that view. In the following pages "homosexuality" is considered to be that historical, cultural phenomenon of human beings' proclivity toward and desire for union with the same sex.

The modern Christian of liberal persuasion no longer considers homosexuality an unspeakable taboo. He is speaking out. He condemns irrational societal prejudice. He worries about unfair employment practices. He wrestles with intolerably hostile military and civil service regulations. He fights for statute reform. He establishes counseling centers. He attends conferences on homosexuality. He even periodically enters into face-to-face dialogue with persons of admitted homosexual proclivity.

The modern moralist has been liberated from the suffocating overlay of what Wainwright Churchill calls our "erotophobic" and "homeophobic" culture. The liberated moralist can now look more realistically into socially deviate sexual behavior patterns that according to Marcuse symbolize an "instinctual freedom in a world of repression." What Christian interested in the future of situational-relational ethics can help but breathe a sigh of ecclesiastical relief— at last, liberation from two hundred long centuries of a Levitical world view!

The Rev. Neale A. Secor is the priest in charge at St. Mary's Episcopal Church in New York City. A former trial lawyer and a graduate of the University of Chicago Law School, he received his theological degree from Union Theological Seminary in New York City. He has coauthored contributions to *The Religious Situation, 1968* and *The Religious Situation, 1969*. Mr. Secor has been involved in various ministries to the new generation and has participated in the work of homophile organizations in San Francisco, Washington, D.C., and New York.

The chapters in the present volume give vigorous and thoughtful evidence of the waning influence of the long era of the old moralistic school of Pipers, Hiltners, Coles, Grimms, Demants ad infinitum who, although different in many ways, saw in homosexuality nothing but a demonic, carnal threat to the very existence of man under the will of God. Supposedly we are no longer irrevocably bound to biblical literalism. D. S. Bailey has lead us out of Sodom by discrediting the alleged homosexual implications of that myth. Other interpreters have revealed the priestly codes in their culture-bound irrelevance for today's world and have reinvestigated Paul's sexual attitudes. The poison of biblical homosexual death penalties has been diluted.

Free at last. Free at last!

Free, however, to what? For what?

Free to join the venerable Helmut Thielicke (*The Ethics of Sex*) and the thoughtful Kimball Jones (*A Christian Understanding of the Homosexual*) so exemplary of the new ethical spirit, in accepting the homosexual into the Christian community for what they claim he is: not an idolater, nor a criminal, nor a leperous outcast; but a genuine product of the "fall," the result of original sin. Free to recognize and accept the awful "burden" of the "constitutional" homosexual's "irreversible situation." Free to help carry this "unnatural expression of human sexuality." Free to help the "absolute invert" realize his "optimal ethical possibilities." Free to understand this "pathology," which like all such pathologies "falls on the same level with abnormal personality structure." Free to help the homosexual man who, after all, is "not responsible for being what he is." Free to feel sorry for, accept, and help this "unnatural" phenomenon of human personality.

It is probably a principle of progress that liberation movements must have their pitfalls and newfound freedoms their limitations. So, the ethical response that moves from thoughtless repression toward enlightened tolerance is no exception. The pitfalls and limitations reflect no discredit on the new freedom or its liberators. But they warrant caution to those who too quickly would buy in the marketplace of ethical freedom only to find that they have purchased but half a loaf. The pitfall of the recent ethical liberation as it regards homosexuality is revealed in the failure to fully come to terms with the implications of relying primarily upon the

Genesis creation myths to define the essential fundamentals of what it means to be "human" in God's image. The limitation upon the ethicist's newfound freedom is his too easy reliance upon questionable psychological data in order to support his definition of sexual humanity.

The modern moralist's thesis of accepting the homosexual appears to be premised upon two basic, if sometimes unelucidated, assumptions. The first is the theological assumption that the homosexual condition is only expressive of the *post-lapsum* deviations from God's essential will. In this instance, it is postulated as a deviation from the God-willed, natural human state of pure maleness or pure femaleness as expressed in Genesis and so is not the subject of particular condemnation. Surely the homosexual is "queer" runs this assumption—but are we not all in some sense deviates from God's pure will and do not all of us therefore participate in the queerness of sin after the fall? The second assumption is the psychological one that the homosexual is mentally ill or "sick"—irreversibly sick like one physically riddled with terminal cancer—and should therefore be encouraged to come to grips with both the liabilities and potentialities of his pathology, but not be ostracized.

Fair enough—certainly better than past ecclesiastical judgments! But what if the assumptions are faulty? Where does that leave the new ethical desire for tolerant acceptance of the homosexual?

I contend that these assumptions are indeed faulty; that the ethical thesis for acceptance of the homosexual as a "sick sinner like the rest of us sick sinners" is, accordingly, questionable; and that we therefore either have to revert to the past—and in some ways more historically honest—posture of moral condemnation, or somehow find new bases for future acceptance.

The elements of the theological problem are clear, if their deliniation elusive. The key is some determinator of the divine will. A requirement of Christian ethics (the "science of human conduct as it is determined by divine conduct"—Brunner) is that human moral decisions should reflect God's will. Catholic moralism—both Roman and Anglican—historically has relied most heavily upon the authoritative tradition of the church as it attempted to define and ascertain the will of God. A rather intricate scheme of values has been developed in the creation of a moral theology. Protestantism, in its search for a Christian ethic, has more often placed reliance upon the biblical word and upon personal faith experience; it has no such worked-out system of moral values for easy reference.

The words of the Bible and the numerical "normalcy" of heterosexuality in the history of human experience provided classical Protestantism with a conception of sexual polarity to be deemed essential to the definition of "human" personality. (By a somewhat different route Catholic moral theology reaches a similar conclusion—e.g., Bailey). Although teachers of Protestant ethics may disagree regarding the treatment of the homosexual, there is no disagreement about his theological nature as a human being. Both the renowned Karl Barth, who had little tolerance for homosexuality, and the able Helmut Thielicke, who has counseled acceptance of the homosexual condition, have a common understanding of God's will of creation as found in the book of Genesis.

So basic is this common understanding of creation in discovering an ethic for human sexuality that I am persuaded it must be dealt with as a condition precedent for reaching an ethic of homosexuality. The temptation of recent moral investigation has been to move on to interpretations of Levitical statutes and of Pauline statements on sexual relations (especially 1 Corinthians 5 and Romans 1), and to overlook the basic assumption upon which such later interpretations rest. It does not suffice to demythologize and liberalize later biblical words without first coming to terms with the biblical assumptions upon which the later words depend —thus, the crucial importance of the Genesis myths of creation.

"Male" he created them. "Female" he created them. And in his own image! Male *and* (a separate) female. Traditional Christian ethics has tended to interpret the conjunctive "and" as a disjunctive "or," so that sexual differentiation has become part of the essential definition of man.

So strong has been this conviction of polarity that it has not only been deemed theologically normative for human relationship (a thou to a thou), but it has also assumed metaphysical significance in the very constitution of "man." To be human becomes, by hypothesis, to be purely male or purely female. Only in monogamous marriage desirous of reproduction is this essential duality preserved in proper balance.

In contrast to this understanding, however, one might recall that also in biblical mythology Adam ("man") was created by God prior to Eve's separation from Adam; one might therefore postulate that the "essential" quality of the God-desired image is a mixture, or combination, of both sexes rather than a strict sexual duality. One might urge that, although the Genesis stories point to an *existential* biological separation of sexual relational *function*, the *essential* mythological separation was of the androgynous "male-female" Adam from God, and not Eve from Adam.

One might continue this corrective process by delving into the rather late times when the Genesis traditions were formed for a greater appreciation of the then cultural needs of the monogamous agrarian family unit, the real fear of Canaanite and other apostate idolatrous sexual-religious practices, the primitive reverence for the semen, and the biological misunderstandings regarding the conception and birth processes. Such investigation might reveal a perspective into which to place the Genesis traditions.

One might even suggest to the liberal ethical interpreter that to equate functional sex differences with essential being is to resort to a literalist biblical anthropology which not only is inappropriate and perhaps completely meaningless in modern discussion, but also is embarrassingly inapposite to his otherwise nonliteralistic ethical methodology.

These suggested possibilities of biblical interpretation must be left to those more interested and skilled in pure hermeneutics.

It well may be revealed by further work by those scholars that Genesis does indeed presume an essential, God-willed strict polarity between male and female, and not just a God-willed functional, relational differentiation. It even may be that a literal interpretation of the Genesis myth will be considered primary for a firm foundation for ethics. It must suffice to say that these are issues of biblical interpretation not fully considered by otherwise thoughtful explorers into the ethical content of homosexuality, even though they are very much considered by the very same explorers when they treat the ethics of heterosexuality! At this point, conclusions simply have been drawn too hastily from predetermined biblical assumptions.

Should an understanding of the Genesis myth requiring an essential male "or" female polarity be agreed upon, ethical students in the days of study ahead must still face the next ethical issue: whether the failure of persons to rejoin as man and woman in monogamous marriage (*henosis*) for the presumed purpose of propagation is a sin which is susceptible to easy Christian "acceptance."

The resolution of this issue is of concern to more persons than just those with homosexual preferences. It is of concern to the bachelor, the unmarried woman, the divorced person, the separated couple, the widow, the widower, and to those young people who in increasing numbers are "living together" or who after a sanctified marriage purposely decide to remain childless. The resolution of this issue likewise has consequences for the behavior patterns of masturbation, sexual abstinence, premarital relationships, extramarital relationships, and nonmarital relationships. Are all of these relationships and all of these sexual practices— along with a gender identification and behavior which prefers the same sex—results of the fall? Are only monogamous child-filled relationships expressive of God's essential divine will for man in relationship? And what might be the status of a thesis like Norman Pittenger's that to be human *means* to be a "lover" and not merely a heterosexual acting-out identifiable object?

Having considered the first leg of Protestant authority, the biblical word, what must we say of the second, the authority of human faith experiences? This authority of personal, cultural experience, as it informs an understanding of homosexual relationships and practices, is instructive in understanding the other nonhenotic practices and relationships as well.

Other writers in this book have set forth in some detail historical, cultural, biological, and anthropological data regarding homosexuality. Within the detail two parallel themes of experiential expression are relevant for our discussion here: (1) Throughout history, the Western church (and in consequence the legal and social codes derived therefrom) has said a loud "No" to homosexuality. (2) Throughout primitive and recorded history, animal life (including human) and certain entire cultures have said either a loud "Yes" or at least an audible "Maybe" to homosexuality.

That many leaders of history, Christian and non-Christian, past and present, have been, or are, homosexually inclined and active hardly validates homosexuality as an ethical possibility. But neither do ecclesiastical injunctions or moral laws eliminate actual homosexual proclivity and behavior. The facts of the historical matter are that homosexuality is a human social phenomenon, has always been so, and has always received cultural recognition, whether pejoratively or positively. The Western church has condemned, and the Western state has outlawed; but the cultural phenomenon itself has continued into the present quite unabated.

One is struck not so much with the efforts to eradicate this human propensity as with its dogged capacity to persist and even flourish in the face of such efforts. This awareness is not at all dissimilar to the repeated confessions of modern-day churchmen about how surprised they are at the "normalcy" of the homosexually inclined persons they have come to know as persons rather than as clinical entities or pastoral charges.

I am not at all sure how much weight should be given this experiential, historical evidence as over against (if that finally be the conclusion) a contrary biblical imperative of sexual polarity in the Genesis myth. I am convinced, however, that it must be accorded some weight as ethical authority in attempting to elicit and comprehend what it means to be human in the divine image and what God's will is for modern man. We simply cannot ignore what the social scientists, cultural historians, anthropologists, and modern-day investigators have been attempting to tell us about homosexuality. At least we cannot ignore this data unless we conclude, a priori, that such human experience and investigation are outside the realm of the divine will. And this I am hesitant to do.

In the realm of "social" or "community" ethics, such data rather than being ignored usually is accorded a high priority as expressive of God's continuing action in history. Within the realm of "personal" ethics, however, there appears to have been a much greater difficulty in giving credence to any authority outside of biblical interpretation, or (as will be discussed below) psychiatric studies.

At this point in the ethical investigation of homosexuality, one cannot state with any assurance whether or not the authority of human historical experience will affront the authority of biblical interpretation. More work, much more work and thinking, needs to be done.

Until it is done, however, the moralist who would accept the homosexual on the theological assumption that he is just another post-lapsum sinner might best pull up his ethical reigns a bit. It might well be that the homosexual, as traditionally has been held in Protestant ethics, is not just "another" sinner, but rather an idolater of the first order who is thwarting the very divine purpose of essential humanity as pure male or pure female joined together in monogamous reproductivity. On the other hand, that might not be the essential quality of "man" as God's likeness at all; or even if it is, it might be understood differently in the light of God-given historical experiences of homosexual patterns and practices.

The one area of human experience to which the "acceptance" ethicist has given close attention is psychology, or at least psychiatry. In fact a strong assumption underlying the plea that Christians "accept" the homosexual is that he is mentally ill. One suspects that in his efforts to come to terms with nonheterosexually oriented persons, the moralist of liberal persuasion has become a bit enamored with psychiatry and has perhaps given that modern field of human understanding an undeservedly high-priestly place in his conclusions.

This chapter is not the place for a full discussion of the various emotional theories regarding homosexuality or of the value systems of the professional psychiatrists which undergird those theories. That can be left to the reader's evaluation of such as Thomas Szasz. It is the place, however, to remind ourselves, as Rollo May has repeatedly urged, that psychiatrists and therapists *do have* values, that they are socially "conservative" values, and that such values previously are informed and molded by traditional cultural and ethical values. Psychiatric diagnoses and prognoses of homosexually oriented patients are not devoid of a priori ethical values. To the contrary, those values define the very meaning of mental "health" or mental "disease," and usually do so in a highly protected, isolated doctor-patient relationship.

The conclusions of a Dr. Bieber (or Hadden, or Ellis, or Erikson, or Berg, or Allen, or the many others) that the homosexual is mentally "ill" must be put into the perspective of Bieber's own admission that "all psychoanalytic theories *assume* that adult homosexuality is pathological," even though the various theories differ because they "assign differing weights to constitutional and experiential determinants." Freud, of course, made similar assumptions although his psychic phenomenology allowed him to call homosexuality a "symptom" of neurosis rather than the neurosis itself. Irrespective of such nice distinctions, the homosexual remained for Freud pathologically "arrested" or "fixated" at some oral period a long way off from healthy maturation.

Certainly the psychiatric diagnoses of homosexuality must be, by hypothesis, pathologically determined. The question for the psychiatrist is not whether a person of homosexual proclivity is mentally sick. He assumes that. His question, rather, is What kind of mental disease is it, and can it be cured?

For the Christian ethicist to rely, therefore, upon the psychiatrist's "findings" that a homosexual is mentally ill or in a "constitutional," "irreversible" pathological state, and therefore to conclude that the homosexual should be "accepted" as such is questionable. What the ethicist is doing in such reliance is basing his assumptions upon the psychiatrist's assumptions, when the psychiatrist originally received his assumptions (values) from the very ecclesiastical ethical predecessors from whom the ethicist feels he is liberally departing. This not only is tautologist reasoning and circuitous investigation; it also participates in a kind of understanding which simply is not helpful to ethical inquiry.

A particular psychiatric theory of homosexual pathology or a particular therapist's etiological findings regarding a particular disturbed person of homosexual orientation hopefully will continue to be helpful to the pastoral counselor. This, however, is not the issue of ethical theory and formulation. The moral issue is with the *nature* of homosexuality, so that the ethical promulgator might better determine whether or not such nature and the personal decisions made therefrom accord with or deviate from what he perceives to be God's will for men in relationships.

In helping to identify the ethical nature of personhood in general, or the nature of homosexual personhood in particular, psychiatric theory continues basically to be enculturated ethical theory in different dress using different labels. Alleged theoretical differences that have little or no logical distinction when placed under the microscope of cultural data investigation are not limited to ethics and psychiatry. Regarding homosexuality, the same process has occurred between Christian ethics and the law. One is hard put to find real distinction between the "sin" of homosexual behavior and the "crime" of homosexual behavior. The labels are different and the sanctions are different, but the nature of both the ethical sin and legal crime of homosexuality are as similar as its alleged mental "illness." Labels do not make fundamental distinctions in value hypotheses and assumptions.

No profession or field of human investigation is of course without its values and prior unconscious assumptions. Sociology, cultural anthropology, and psychology must be included with law and psychiatry. There is a difference, however. The difference is that psychiatry like religion and the law does not—or at least should not—hold itself out as attempting to be "scientifically objective." The political and healing professions of a society require active values and beliefs to bring to the political and healing processes. The behavioral social sciences of sociology—including cultural anthropology—and psychology, however, do attempt to fulfill the task of ascertaining objective data for the sake of intellectual and scientific purity, much the same way that physics and biochemistry do in the physical sciences. Application of the data of scientific conclusions to specific problems is some-one else's job. It is within these two behavioral fields, therefore, that one concerned with ethical foundations receives clues as to the nature of the issue with which he is concerned.

Within this perspective Evelyn Hooker's findings based on clini-cally objective testings, that there are no observable psychologi-cal differences between homosexually and heterosexually ori-ented men except their gender-object preferences, and that therefore as a "clinical entity" homosexuality is "neutral" and *not* pathological are of unusual ethical pertinence. Of similar rele-vance and pertinence are the related social-psychology findings of Pomeroy and Simon and Gagnon.

These and related anthropological studies lend support to the behaviorist belief that society itself and not the homosexual basi-cally is the "sick" patient which in its illness "causes" persons to "become" homosexually oriented—so, in varying degrees and emphases, with the studies of Lindner, Marcuse, Churchill, Mead, Malinowski, Beach, Benedict, Weinberg, Kardiner, Van den Haag, Ruitenbeek, et al. England's famous "Wolfenden Report" follows Hooker and others in the conclusion that there is no medically scientific basis for homosexuality as a separate clinical entity.

Whichever tack one prefers to take, a thesis that holds out the homosexual as irrevocably mentally ill and therefore ethically concludes that he should be accepted as such, ignores to its peril much scientifically informed data.

As with the theological assumptions discussed above, the present failure of psychiatry to provide an unassailable standard of psychic health does not mean that, upon further investigation, homosexuality may not be found to be a historical, cultural (and psychological) aberration of a pathological (diseased) nature. And I certainly am not implying that there are not many emotionally disturbed persons who are otherwise homosexually inclined. What I am arguing is that at this point of initial inquiry into the human experience of homosexuality there simply are too few data cards on the table of honest investigation, and that the cards which are revealed point in diverse and often conflicting directions. The only fact that appears with some certainty is that homosexual identification and practice are learned in the human growth process, much the same way as are all personality identifications and practices. Definite conclusions, ethical or otherwise, simply cannot be made upon the available data.

Let us suppose for a moment, however, that a future consensus should be reached in the position that homosexual propensity is an uncontrollable disorder of the basic psychic nature of man, and not merely a deviation from the social sexual patterning of the majority of persons. The Protestant moralist remains faced with at least three more fairly basic questions prior to making definitive conclusions: What place should ethics give to such a psychiatric consensus within the experiential authority referents for deciding God's will for man's sexual being and behavior? If the consensus is given a priority place, then will Christian ethics "accept" *all* homosexually inclined persons, or only those constitutional *in*verts who have no choice in the matter but not the willful *per*verts? If only the *in*verts are accepted, then is Protestant ethics participating in a moral theology of a gradation of sins (material-venial vs. formal-mortal) more acceptable in Catholic than Protestant tradition?

Understanding and appreciation should be accorded honest Christian motivations behind the desire to forgive and accept downtrodden minorities. It is an admirable desire. Caution likewise should be accorded lest these motivations partake in questionable hypotheses and thus stand to open to Camus' reflection that the "welfare of the people . . . has always been an alibi of tyrants, and it provides the further advantage of giving the servants of tyranny a good conscience."

As indicated at the outset these pages have been argumentative and exploratory rather than definitive; they have raised more questions than they have provided answers; they have offered more criticisms than they have constructive suggestions. I have deliberately assumed this argumentative, critical, question-raising role in the firm belief that this is the appropriate ethical stance at this stage of inquiry regarding the ethics of homosexuality. I am impressed by a Christian history of near obsession with sexual issues and therefore am requesting that, regarding the specific issue of homosexuality, we draw a halt on making hasty theological-ethical conclusions, particularly when they appear founded on untested assumptions and incomplete data.

It probably is the case that, in this particular arena of human conduct, the Christian church has been thrown from its accustomed role of teacher and into that of learner. The learning posture understandably is awkward and at times abrasive, perhaps especially so for those accustomed to promulgating ethical theory and positions. It is a necessary posture, however, if the Christian community is to overcome the oppression and repression of the homosexual minority for which it has primary historical responsibility, deal with the collective guilt resulting from that responsibility, and then move on to an ethical stance which is both intelligible to and workable for the homosexual and churchman alike.

In the learning process we are not left bereft of starting points and working hypotheses. The starting points of honest biblical reinterpretation and open investigation into the human historical experience of homosexuality as recorded by the social sciences are obvious ones if Protestantism is to take seriously its traditional ethical authority referents. A third starting point would be for today's Christian to test his present faith understanding of man against the reality referent of the homosexual himself; this might be accomplished by many more personal meetings and confrontations between the Christian and the homosexual in dialogue settings or within the homosexual subcultures.

I would further suggest that, until proved inadequate or incorrect, the following tentative working hypotheses provide an ethical framework during the learning process:

1. All human sexual identifications and behavior patterns, irre-

spective of desired gender object, are morally neutral; i.e., avoid making prior ethical judgments regarding sexual behavior on the basis of the *object* of sexual drives alone.

2. No matter what the particular sexual behavior (hetero, homo, mono), the test for sin is whether or not that behavior meets presently understood and approved Christian standards (what God wills for man) for all human relational behavior; i.e., avoid making prior ethical judgments regarding sin on the basis of *sexual* behavior alone.

3. Christian ethical concern for the homosexual exists not because he has a certain sexual proclivity but because he is a person; i.e., avoid making prior ethical judgments regarding concern for people on the basis of *socially aberrant* behavior alone.

I am aware that these suggested working hypotheses can be stereotyped—positively or negatively—as mere tenants of the so-called new morality. They are suggested, however, not as truths or tenants of anything. Rather, they are working hypotheses; and if certain aspects of the new morality provide an open-ended framework for further ethical inquiry into the nature of homosexuality and homosexual behavior, so be it. It is exactly that open-endedness for which I have been arguing.

sex
laws

CHAPTER 7

The Need for Homosexual Law Reform

GILBERT M. CANTOR

While it is nowhere unlawful to be "a homosexual," whatever that may be, the basic illegality of homosexual behavior is the behavior proscribed in all states but one by the sodomy laws. For the offense of sodomy, the states provide a vast array of punishments, as shown on page 84.

In this "crazy-quilt" pattern, we notice that penalties range from a maximum of one year in New York to possible life imprisonment in California, Idaho, Missouri, Montana, and Nevada. Thirteen states have maximum first-offense penalties less than life but at least twenty years, while another twenty-three have maximums ranging from ten to fifteen years. Several states provide a five-year maximum term, while others provide a five-year minimum. In ten states a fine may be imposed as an alternative to imprisonment, while two states prescribe both fine and a jail term.

If we search out a "recent trend" in legislative attention to penalties for sodomy, we discover that in the period from 1951 to 1965 Arizona, California, New Hampshire, New Jersey, and Wyoming increased their penalties, while Arkansas, Colorado, Georgia, Illinois, Nevada, North Dakota, New York, Oregon, and Wisconsin lessened theirs.[1]

The sodomy laws themselves, apart from their penalties, have two characteristics which merit attention. The first is that while

---

Mr. Gilbert M. Cantor is a member of the Philadelphia law firm of Goodis, Greenfield, Narin & Mann. He is a graduate of Harvard Law School and the author of the book *The Barnes Foundation: Reality vs. Myth.* Mr. Cantor has served as counsel to homophile organizations, written articles and lectured on legal aspects of homosexuality, and has participated in legal disputes and litigation involving homosexuality.

THE PENALTIES FOR SODOMY

Maximum fine and/or imprisonment for first offense unless otherwise noted. When two numbers are given, they represent minimum and maximum penalties.

STATE	PENALTY	STATE	PENALTY
Alabama	2–10 years	Missouri	2 years–life
Alaska	1–10 years	Montana	5 years–life
Arizona	5–20 years	Nebraska	20 years
Arkansas	1–21 years	Nevada	1 year–life
California	1 year–life	New Hampshire	$1000 or 5 years or both
Colorado	1–14 years		
Connecticut	30 years	New Jersey	$5000 or 20 years or both
Delaware	$1000 & 3 years		
Dist. of Col.	$1000 or 10 years	New Mexico	$5000 or 2–10 years or both
Florida	20 years	New York	$500 or 1 year or both
Georgia	1–10 years 2nd conviction, 10–30 years	North Carolina	Discretionary
		North Dakota	10 years
Hawaii	$1000 & 20 years	Ohio	1–20 years
		Oklahoma	10 years
Idaho	5 years–life	Oregon	15 years
Illinois		Pennsylvania	$5000 or 10 years or both
Indiana	$100–$1000 or 2–14 years or both	Rhode Island	7–20 years
		South Carolina	$500 to ? or 5 years or both
Iowa	10 years	South Dakota	10 years
Kansas	10 years	Tennessee	5–15 years
Kentucky	2–5 years	Texas	2–15 years
Louisiana	$2000 or 5 years or both	Utah	3–20 years
		Vermont	1–5 years
Maine	1–10 years	Virginia	1–3 years
Maryland	1–10 years	Washington	10 years
Massachusetts	20 years	West Virginia	1–10 years
Michigan	15 years	Wisconsin	$500 or 5 years or both
Minnesota	20 years		
Mississippi	10 years	Wyoming	10 years

these laws have been applied almost exclusively to homosexual behavior, the laws make no distinction in terms as between heterosexual and homosexual acts, a fact reminiscent of the famous observation of Anatole France that the law prohibits rich and poor alike to sleep on the park benches.

The other characteristic of what we have been calling the sodomy laws is that the prohibitions are variously expressed. The laws are not uniform as to the particular acts which are punishable. While some states use the term sodomy, some refer to the crime against nature and others employ the word buggery. These terms are used singly or in combination with one another or with such additional expressions as unnatural intercourse, lascivious act, carnal copulation, and sexual perversion.[2]

Where the prohibitions are not specific, some courts have construed these laws as applying only to intercourse per anus (the common-law meaning of sodomy), while others have held the prohibitions to embrace copulation per os, or fellatio. Twenty states have sodomy laws which have been framed to enlarge the common-law definition.

The impact of these laws, of course, varies with the attitudes of prosecutors, judges, and juries. Moreover, for persons accused, the exposure of arrest and trial may be at least as damaging as actual conviction,[3] and often calamitous.[4]

On the other hand, it must be noted that while the sodomy laws are by no means a dead letter, and indeed underlie and support other forms of adverse treatment of and attitudes toward homosexuals, by far the greatest criminal law involvement of homosexuals occurs under laws proscribing solicitation, disorderly conduct, lewd and lascivious behavior, and vagrancy.[5] Accordingly, Martin Hoffman is quite correct in observing that "homosexual law reform must mean something more than merely the abolition of the sodomy laws, or it will mean nothing." [6]

The case for homosexual law reform, which is the burden of this chapter, involves the sodomy laws themselves and also the laws under which homosexuals may be arrested for soliciting or even "loitering to solicit." We shall consider first the reasons for abolishing the sodomy laws, a step recommended in the two major studies of such legislation, that of the American Law Institute (whose recommendation was adopted by Illinois in its adoption of the Model Penal Code) and that of the English Committee on Homosexual Offenses and Prostitution (the Wolfenden Committee), whose 1957 recommendation was adopted after ten years of public debate.

(The major policy reason for abolishing the sodomy laws is simply that acts committed in private by consenting adults [7] are matters of private morality and not properly the concern of the state.)

The Wolfenden Committee concluded that the function of the criminal law in the fields under its study is "to preserve order and decency, to protect the citizen from what is offensive and injurious, and to provide sufficient safeguards against the exploitation and corruption of others, particularly those who are specially vulnerable because they are young, weak in body or mind, inexperienced, or in a state of special physical, official, or economic dependence." On the other hand, said the report, "There must remain a realm of private morality and immorality which is, in brief and crude terms, not the law's business." [8]

The American Law Institute, in similar vein, observed: "No harm to the secular interest of the community is involved in atypical sex practice in private between consenting adult partners. This area of private morals is the distinctive concern of spiritual authorities." [9]

These expressions, of course, were foreshadowed and influenced by the position of John Stuart Mill, who wrote in *On Liberty:*

> The only purpose for which power can rightfully be exercised over any member of a civilized community against his will is to prevent harm to others. . . . His own good either physical or moral is not a sufficient warrant. He cannot rightfully be compelled to do or forbear because it will be better for him to do so, because it will make him happier, because in the opinion of others, to do so would be wise or even right.[10]

While this "ultra vires" argument of the American Law Institute and of the Wolfenden Committee was aimed toward a legislative remedy, the policy involved rises, in the American system, to the constitutional level. Moreover, while constitutional considerations are not foreclosed to our legislative bodies, and indeed ought to be matters of legislative concern in cases of substantial constitutional doubt, there are certain advantages which would flow from a Supreme Court pronouncement that the sodomy laws are unconstitutional. Those advantages are principally two: (1) the fact that a single Supreme Court edict affects fifty states simultaneously, and (2) the "educational" impact of the Supreme Court's resolution of such an issue (for which the disposition of the "separate but equal" doctrine in the *Brown* case is the best recent example).

Built into our Constitution, happily, are certain fundamental notions such as "due process" and "cruel and unusual punishment," which are, in Professor Gottlieb's phrase, "issues with leverage." [11] These issues involve rights which rise and expand, leavened by the yeast of our evolving humanity, while our knowledge and values are influenced, reciprocally, by the Court's expansion of those rights.

Where our concern with a particular kind of law, such as the sodomy law, is substantially a concern with its side effects— behavior and attitudes which the law supports, apart from the direct application of the law itself—the leverage or educational impact of a Supreme Court decision is at a premium.

The constitutional argument, necessarily expressed for the purpose of this chapter in highly condensed form, may be stated as follows:

1. While the federal government operates under its "delegated" (though greatly expanded) powers, the states legislate in accordance with the powers reserved to them, principally the "police powers," which are the powers to legislate in the interest of public health and safety (in various formulations), including "preservation of good order and public morals." [12] While the scope of the police power is very broad, the Court stated as recently as 1962:

> The classic statement of the rule in Lawton vs. Steele, 152 U.S. 133, 137 (1894) is still valid today: "To justify the state in . . . interposing its authority in behalf of the public, it must appear first, that the interests of the public require such interference; and, second, that the means are reasonably necessary for the accomplishment of the purpose, and not unduly oppressive upon individuals." [13]

Stated another way, "due process" requires that the state's purpose in legislation be a proper public purpose and that the means employed be reasonably calculated to achieve it.[14] It is difficult to perceive a proper public purpose in seeking to punish adults who privately and consensually engage in oral or anal intercourse. Moreover, if there were a proper public purpose for sodomy legislation as such, or as applied to those acts in a homosexual context, surely experience has demonstrated that the sodomy laws may not reasonably be expected to achieve the legislative purpose.

2. The sodomy laws represent an effort to enforce a morality rooted in religion, and, as such, violate the prohibition against the establishment of religion. While most of our principal crimes—murder, robbery, etc.—may be traceable to religious prohibitions, they also involve secular harms: they are not "crimes without victims." [15] Other criminal laws, such as the Sunday laws, though religious in origin, may be found to have acquired a secular purpose or justification. The sodomy laws, in contrast, may be found to be rooted in religion and to have *lost* their secular justification if ever they had one.[16]

As to the religious source of the prohibition, see Leviticus 18:22: "You shall not lie with a male as with a woman." The prohibition evolved into the crime *peccatum illud horrible, inter Christianos non nominandum,* the abominable sin not to be named among Christians,[17] today the "crime against nature," "sodomy," and so on. The word sodomy announces the connection with the city of Sodom where the forbidden practice prevailed, and the references to "unnatural intercourse" and "acts against nature" incorporate the traditional Judeo-Christian concept of "natural law." [18]

The religious (or American religious) aspect is perhaps underscored by the fact that the proscription involved is not common to all civilized nations. The majority of European countries do not prohibit homosexual acts between consenting adults.[19] Where the law reflects notions of morality rooted in our particular history with values derived from biblical sources, and has no clear utilitarian basis,[20] the case is particularly strong for an unconstitutional breach in the wall between church and state.

These two constitutional objections to the sodomy laws, namely, (1) that they exceed the police power of the states, as limited by the concept of "due process," and (2) that they involve the establishment of religion, in violation of the First Amendment (as applied to the states under the Fourteenth), may overlap. As stated by Professor Henkin:

> Perhaps the objection that some morals legislation imposes a religious morality is a facet of the earlier argument that morals legislation cannot be rationally supported. For in substantial part the effect, if not the purpose, of constitutional provisions forbidding religious establishment and guaranteeing the free exercise of religion is also to bar the influence of government in the realm of the nonrational, the sacred precincts, of personal belief, the personal "answer," even personal idiosyncrasy. The domain of government, it is suggested, is that in which social problems are resolved by rational social processes, in which men can reason together, can examine problems and propose solutions capable of objective proof or persuasion, subject to objective scrutiny by courts and electors. I ask whether legislation that is based on a particular religion, even on what is common to many religions, on what is supported by history only, on what is not capable of reasoned consideration and solution, is rendered unto government by the Constitution.[21]

3. A constitutionally protected "right of privacy" was articulated by the Supreme Court in the 1965 case of *Griswold vs. Connecticut*. In April of 1969, in the case of *Stanley vs. Georgia*, the right of privacy was again invoked in a holding that a Georgia statute, insofar as it made mere possession of obscene matter a crime, was unconstitutional. While the Court discussed the "speech" aspects of the case—"the right to receive information and ideas, regardless of their social worth,"—it also upheld the defendant's "right to satisfy his intellectual and *emotional needs* in the privacy of his own home," citing an earlier case which stated that the makers of the Constitution "sought to protect Americans in their beliefs, their thoughts, *their emotions, and their sensations.*" (Italics added.) It would seem to require minimal elasticity for this concept to cover private homosexual acts.

The consideration of the proper limitation of governmental authority in the area of "private morality" as discussed above, whether framed as a matter of policy or in constitutional terms, is only one of several substantial reasons for the abolition of the sodomy laws. Among the significant "justice" reasons and pragmatic reasons for abolition are the following:

1. The sodomy laws are ineffective. Such prohibitions can hardly be expected to change a person's sexual orientation. As in the case of Prohibition, "[If] there is too large a gulf between precept and practice, then the law will not work." [22]

2. The laws are capricious. As we have already noted, laws prohibiting oral and anal copulation are applied principally against such copulation by homosexuals. As to homosexuals, such laws are applied principally against male rather than female homosexuals. As to male homosexuals, it is widely believed—and inherently credible—that persons of means and position are given preferential treatment at each stage of the police and judicial process. Apart from these broad inequities, it is also clear—and here we refer to enforcement of the solicitation-type laws as well as the sodomy law itself—that enforcement varies from time to time and place to place with respect to both the intensity and the quality of detection and enforcement procedures.

3. The law, even when not enforced, has an adverse effect on character and behavior. It has been estimated that between 2 and 5 percent of the total male population of the United States are exclusively homosexual; that 37 percent have experienced some overt homosexual contacts to the point of orgasm since adolescence; and that 95 percent have violated, at some time in their lives, one or more statutes relating to sexual behavior.[23] Under these circumstances, in a society which places a high value on sexual conformity, a substantial part of the population have reason, in their own experience, to fear the weakening of that value system. As Dr. Szasz has pointed out, the homosexual, because he rejects heterosexuality, undermines its value. Thus he threatens society not by his actual behavior but by the symbolic significance of his acts.[24] Society, accordingly, threatened by the felt temptation and the perceived example, labels certain persons as homosexuals, deviants, criminals.

Deviance, it should be recognized, "is *not* a quality of the act the person commits, but rather a consequence of the application by others of rules and sanctions to an 'offender.' The deviant is one to whom that label has been successfully applied; deviant behavior is behavior that people so label." [25] By labeling the deviant, and applying sanctions to go with the label, the social ideal is made clearer by contrast and is made alone to appear desirable. Thus, in order to maintain and dwell in the social paradise of acceptable behavior, we maintain a hell of deviance, to which the homosexual is assigned.[26]

As Schur points out in *Crimes Without Victims,* criminal proceedings are status-degradation ceremonies, but even when the deviant is not publicly identified and officially dealt with, he is aware that his behavior is legally proscribed as well as socially disapproved.

> Sensing that he is different or is doing an unusual act is one thing, feeling that his act is strongly disapproved is another, and knowledge that he has become a lawbreaker yet another. . . . Just as the mere knowledge that he has become a "criminal" may alter the individual's self-image, so, too, may legal proscription drive him into various behavior patterns that reinforce this image and create new problems for himself and for society at large. . . . [The] formation of deviant subcultures, as well as the occurrence of certain types of secondary deviations (including secondary crime), may be crucially related to the criminalization of particular forms of socially disapproved behavior.[27]

④ The sodomy laws provide, both directly and through the support they lend to private sanctions, the opportunity for blackmail of homosexuals, and extortion. These are crimes in which, in contrast to sodomy itself, there is a "victim," and it is a victim who is unlikely to seek the protection of the law.

If we shift our attention from the sodomy laws to the laws under which persons may be prosecuted for soliciting others to commit sodomy, we encounter the phenomena of (1) sporadic enforcement (including harassment), (2) entrapment by "decoys," and (3) the underlying question whether solicitation, without more, should constitute a crime. The underlying question, in turn, has two aspects: (a) whether it should be criminal to solicit an activity which itself should not constitute a crime, and (b) whether such conduct, even if deemed objectionable per se, is a subject worthy of legal proscription and police activity.

The enforcement of the sodomy laws themselves is rare, as we have observed, but it is also sporadic. In the period 1950–54 only 89 cases were reported in the United States, of which 27 were in California, 9 in Texas, and 5 in New York. The prosecution of sodomy obviously bears no particular relationship to the occurrence of it. Perhaps even more uneven is the official treatment of solicitation offenses. Variations occur according to local pressures, personal inclinations of officials, and available police manpower. San Francisco, Washington, D.C., and Miami Beach have been singled out as the centers of harassment arrests. "One Miami and Miami Beach night of raids [of bars] by Dade County Sheriff Tom Kelly led to the arrest of 53 persons, and the raids were conducted on the pretext of checking those arrested for venereal diseases." [28]

Schofield reports this English example. "In 1955 there was one prosecution for importuning in Manchester; in 1956 and 1957 there were none; in 1958 there were two. A new chief constable was appointed at the end of that year and the number of prosecutions for importuning rose to 30 in 1959, to 105 in 1960, to 135 in 1961, and to 216 in 1962." [29]

In the case of the major crimes—for example, homicide, burglary, and robbery—we know that only a relatively small proportion of the "criminals" are detected and convicted, but we assume this to be related in the main to the effectiveness of the police in each locality and not to considerations of expediency, prejudice, or politics.

Where, on the other hand, as in the case of sodomy and solicitation, the laws from jurisdiction to jurisdiction reflect a kaleidoscopic variety, where the chance of an "offender" being caught and sent to prison is probably less than one in many thousands, and where the enforcement efforts vary widely from time to time and from place to place, such laws and their enforcement betray irrational elements and smack of the persecution of a minority group.

The principal mode of enforcement, the police "decoy," does little to detract from that impression. The decoy is a police officer who dresses and behaves in a manner presumably attractive to homosexuals, frequents the places where homosexual solicitation may be anticipated, elicits a solicitation, and makes an arrest. He is frequently reinforced by another officer who stays out of sight but appears when the arrest is made. Dr. Hoffman has urged persuasively that "putting out as decoys police officers who are young, attractive, and seductively dressed, and who engage in enticing conversations with homosexuals, is itself an outrage to public decency." [30]

Beyond our moral-aesthetic response to this particular police enterprise lies also the more technical issue of entrapment. Entrapment is police activity designed to foster rather than to prevent crime; where the intent to commit the crime originates in the mind of the officer, not the defendant, there is entrapment.[31]

As the transaction leading to the arrest is necessarily private in almost all cases, and even the arresting officer's cohort cannot ordinarily come near enough to be a corroborating witness, the decision in particular cases as to whether or not entrapment has occurred depends on whether the officer's testimony or that of the defendant is believed. Homosexuals frequently claim entrapment and police ordinarily insist that the practice is avoided. While the frequency of entrapment cannot be asserted with any assurance, and while all persons are entitled to a presumption of innocence for purposes of criminal prosecution, we cannot stultify ourselves with the assumption that the police, whose excesses have been established in other areas, such as interrogation procedures and the use of force, are always or even generally able to resist the entrapment temptation in the secretive exchanges in which the arrangement to engage in sodomy takes place.

Apart from the questions of sporadic enforcement or entrapment, there is the more basic consideration as to whether solicitation should be a crime. If it is agreed that the sodomy laws should be annulled, on constitutional or public policy grounds, the question, at one level, is why it should be unlawful to request an act which it is lawful to perform.

If it is answered that the solicitation, when refused, involves an annoyance which is either absent or forgiven when the solicitation is accepted, we are then confronted with the question whether this, among the many annoyances of civilized life, should be deemed worthy of legal (criminal law) attention. There are several reasons why it should not be.

In the first place, the solicitation of sexual encounters is a very common occurrence, and in most cases we are content—if not a little more than content—with the option of saying No.

Second, we should weigh against the annoyance involved the fact that the real (the extra-legal) punishment frequently has a calamitous effect on the person arrested, an effect far beyond what the law itself provides, so that the penalty is necessarily disproportionate to the offense; and thus an exposure to a "cruel and unusual punishment" is, in effect, built into the criminal process in this kind of case.

Third, as the soliciting persons in most cases make their inquiries by words, looks, or gestures which would go unnoticed by most heterosexuals, as almost all arrests result from the activity of decoys and not from complaints of other persons, and as we have other more serious activities requiring police attention, it is, in Dr. Hoffman's words, "a very good question just why public funds are being expended for this purpose." [32]

Even if it should be thought desirable, apart from these considerations, to keep on the books a law proscribing solicitation, surely any such law *should by definition exclude any solicitation in which the complaining party is a police officer.* If preservation of the "king's peace" is thought to require protection of citizens from unwanted sexual solicitation, surely this interest does not extend to persons, such as police decoys, who approach homosexuals *in order to be solicited.*

What we have then, in summary, are laws which (1) involve an activity in which no one is demonstrably harmed and in which the state has no proper interest; (2) have no realistic chance of deterring the activity toward which they are addressed; (3) involve in their enforcement tremendous and disproportionate harm to persons arrested and prosecuted; (4) lend support to private sanctions and biased attitudes toward homosexuals generally; (5) have an adverse influence on the character and behavior of homosexuals; (6) provide the opportunity for the commission of other crimes, such as blackmail and extortion, with respect to which police protection cannot ordinarily be sought; and (7) are the subject of capricious enforcement efforts and encourage obnoxious police practices in a highly undesirable allocation of our limited police resources. These considerations, principally, make out the "case" for homosexual law reform.

CHAPTER 8

The Law & the Church vs. the Homosexual

LEWIS I. MADDOCKS

During the autumn of 1967, I took a three-month sabbatical from my regular job to study the civil liberties problems facing the homosexual in America. The conclusions of that study were the subject of a paper which was published at the end of the year.[1] In the article, the church was challenged to take certain actions leading toward the removal of much of the ignorance and mythology surrounding the nature of homosexuality and also to influence the removal of the many injustices our laws and governmental policies inflict on this greatly misunderstood minority. Among the recommendations suggested were such proposals as the holding of conferences, seminars, and workshops on the nature of homosexuality, compiling background materials for the conferences, as well as invitations to homosexuals to participate, plus other ways of educating the public in general and persons of special concern, such as parish ministers, and military chaplains in particular.

In addition to these educational recommendations, there was a special appeal to the church to use its influence to (1) bring about the repeal of laws which make homosexual practices between consenting adults in private a crime (which is the current situation

Dr. Lewis I. Maddocks is a political scientist and the executive director of the Council for Christian Social Action, United Church of Christ. A specialist in constitutional law, Dr. Maddocks taught political science for fourteen years before coming to CCSA, most recently at the College of Wooster, Wooster, Ohio. He has contributed many articles to UCC magazines. He spent a sabbatical leave studying the problems of law and civil liberties involved in the case of the homosexual.

in every state except Illinois), (2) end police practices of enticement and entrapment in the enforcement of laws against solicitation by homosexuals, (3) end the federal government's policy of
denying security clearances to all homosexuals and totally excluding them from federal employment and all branches of the
armed services. Finally, I recommended that the church cease
whatever internal policies of discrimination it practices against
homosexuals in admission to seminaries, ordination, and full
membership into the life of the church.

Although the study taught me much about the nature of homosexuality and the problems of homosexuals vis-à-vis state laws
and federal policies, even more was learned from the hostile
reactions of many persons to my recommendations. It has become abundantly clear that much more needs to be done to
eliminate the tremendous amount of mythology which surrounds
homosexuality. The two sets of recommendations dealing with the
changing of laws and federal policies on the one hand and the
changing of its internal policies on the other should be among the
major concerns of the church if the nature of homosexuality is to
be understood and if injustices toward homosexuals are to be
eliminated.

Laws and Federal Policies

In matters of public policy, the homosexual is the victim of
discrimination in several areas. Those which are particularly serious are (1) the laws against consensual homosexual practices
between adults and the methods used to enforce them, (2) the
policy by the federal government of total exclusion of homosexuals from government employment and from access to security
clearances, and (3) the complete rejection of homosexuals from
induction or enlistment in the armed forces.

The homosexual and the law. A thorough discussion of the
laws relating to homosexuality would include a description of a
great variety of state and local laws dealing with a myriad of
sexual acts known by vastly different names and invoking great
discrepancies in degrees of punishment for their violation. Such
is not the purpose of this chapter. Here the concern is limited to
laws against homosexual practices between consenting adults in
private, the methods used to enforce laws against solicitation for

homosexual purposes, and certain policies of the federal government.

The leaders of homophile organizations, and homosexuals generally, are not opposed to laws which are designed to protect persons from sexual coercion, to protect children and youths from sexual exploitation, and to protect society from public displays of sexual behavior. Laws against rape and violations of public decency are supported whether the character of the sexual act is homosexual or heterosexual. By the same token, wholesale and overt acts of solicitation for homosexual purposes are to be deplored as much as similar acts for heterosexual purposes. But laws against homosexual acts between consenting adults in private should be repealed and police enforcement of laws against solicitation should be carried out without resort to enticement and entrapment procedures.

The most famous proposal for repeal of laws making homosexual acts between consenting adults in private illegal is that of the Wolfenden Committee in England which states in its report:

> Unless a deliberate attempt is made by society, acting through the agency of the law, to equate the sphere of crime with that of sin, there must remain a realm of private morality and immorality which is, in brief and crude terms, not the law's business. To say this is not to condone or encourage private immorality. On the contrary, to emphasize the personal and private nature of moral or immoral conduct is to emphasize the personal and private responsibility of the individual for his actions, and that is a responsibility which a mature agent can properly be expected to carry for himself without the threat of punishment from the law.[2]

A major result of the work done by the Wolfenden Committee was the repeal in 1967 of the law in England making homosexual acts between consenting adults in private a crime. In the United States, the American Law Institute exempted such laws from its Model Penal Code in 1955.[3] In 1961, Illinois became the only state in the nation to repeal laws against such acts when committed by consenting adults in private. At the meetings of the Ninth International Congress on Criminal Law in 1965, similar views were adopted.[4]

In a most informative study on the enforcement and administration of laws dealing with homosexuality in Los Angeles County, the authors concluded that adult, consensual homosexual practices involve neither sexual coercion of adults nor sexual exploitation of children, even when occurring publicly, and when occurring privately, do not "invade any of the objective societal interests protected by law" and thus "only *public* displays of consensual homosexuality should be the legitimate concern of the criminal law." [5]

Just as the leaders of homophile groups and homosexuals generally do not object to laws which protect children and youths, and which respect public decency as well as forbid the use of force, they also support law enforcement methods which observe the principles of fairness and due process. What is objected to and does demand reform are those practices of some police officers which involve attempts to obtain arrests through enticement and entrapment of persons suspected of being homosexuals. Jess Stern states that according to homosexuals, "Of the thousands of homosexuals arrested for soliciting, more than half were entrapment victims picked up by police who flirted with them in parks, movie houses, subways." [6] Although such practices have been virtually abandoned in some cities, especially in New York, Washington, and San Francisco, they are not uncommon in some other areas. The form such enticement and entrapment may take varies from the use of police as decoys dressed to look like the more flamboyant homosexuals, who actually make the initial proposition, to less obvious methods in which plainclothesmen frequent homosexual hangouts and arrest anyone who makes the proposition to them. The former practice finds few defenders. Many judges will throw a case out of court that involves a defendant who has been arrested as a result of such tactics. The latter type of entrapment is defended by many police officers on the ground that such arrests take place only in areas where there is considerable human traffic and opportunity for soliciting. The homosexuals, on the other hand, point out that soliciting is done in such a way that it is rarely a threat to public decency. Even when the homosexual makes the initial proposition, it is done discreetly by an invitation to have a drink or accompany him to his room, or even by small talk while he tries to determine whether or not he is talking to a prospective sexual partner. Any non-homosexual who is so approached need only indicate his lack of interest in the proposition. Certainly women do this all the time when approached by heterosexual males without anyone suggesting such males ought to be arrested.

Another example of a law-enforcement method which should be curtailed is the use of tactics intended to harass homosexuals. Frequent police raids on "gay" bars, constant and conspicuous surveillance of such places, and revocation of liquor licenses of restaurants where homosexuals congregate are only some of the means used to close them down as menaces "to public morals and welfare." In some localities, such practices are flagrant whereas in others the courts are opposing them. In late 1967, the New Jersey Supreme Court overruled New Jersey's State Alcoholic Beverage Commission when it revoked the liquor license of bars for permitting apparent homosexuals to congregate in them.[7] The Court ruled that homosexuals "have the undoubted right to congregate in public as long as their behavior conforms with currently acceptable standards of decency and morality."

Other examples of law enforcement methods against homosexuals are the compiling of lists of names of known and suspected homosexuals (who are interrogated at length, which results in additional names for use whenever there is a concerted drive to suppress homosexuality in a community), and registration of certain types of sex offenders with the police. These practices raise serious questions of constitutionality relative to self-incrimination and possible disclosure of information to unauthorized persons. The UCLA study refers to this practice of registration wherein the authors state:

> The reasons for requiring registration of consensual homosexuals are not altogether clear. Some enforcement officials feel that the requirement for registration is itself effective as a deterrent to homosexual activity. This is questionable, however, because the threat of penalties ranging from one year in the county jail for misdemeanors, to fifteen years for oral copulation, to an indeterminate sentence for sodomy, does not seem to deter homosexuals. Another argument in favor of registration is that it aids enforcement by providing a readily available index to "sex criminals" residing in a given area and facilitates investigation of sex crimes. However, most officials agree that there are so many registrants that it is impractical to check each one. . . . Enforcement officials who favor registration do so

on the assumption that homosexuals are prone to commit violent crimes and crimes against children. But even if this is true, the registration system is unwieldy and does not aid enforcement. If only those homosexuals who committed crimes involving children or violence were registered, the police would have a smaller number of persons to investigate and the information would have a marked utility. Thus the registration system, as it currently exists, is not justified as an aid in enforcement.[8]

A final area of concern over law-enforcement practices is in the use of police peepholes and two-way mirrors in public rest rooms. The right of privacy is a right too sacred to be ignored; thus such practices as these have brought non-homosexuals to the side of homophile organizations in their attempts to bring such forms of police surveillance to an end. As in the case of many civil liberties issues, it is a matter of balancing interests: the interest of the police to protect the public against homosexual solicitation and behavior in places of public accommodation versus the right of privacy for all persons to use public rest rooms without being observed. The most reasonable solution would seem to be frequent patrolling by police that would prevent homosexual practices from taking place in public. By patrol enforcement methods, the right of privacy is observed and the protection of public decency is maintained.

In conclusion, one psychoanalyst has made clear his views regarding the wisdom of laws against homosexuality. In his view, prohibitive laws will not reduce the occurrence of homosexuality; in fact such laws do more harm than good. He writes:

> The actual effects of the prohibition of homosexuality certainly outweigh any likely benefit. Both homosexuals and heterosexuals are worse off psychologically. The law creates an occasion for blackmail; certainly this is justifiable only if the law is effective, if it is necessary, or at least useful, and if violators could abstain from violation. If at least one of these conditions were fulfilled, one might argue for the law. But, as has been indicated above, none are. On the other hand, the opportunity for blackmail not only harasses those subject to it, but it corrupts those taking advantage of it, and specially those charged with enforcement of

the law. The actual effects of the law are thus an unmitigated evil.[9]

In all the discussion of the homosexual and the law, it is often stated that laws against adult consensual activities in private are not usually enforced and that usually only minor fines are invoked. This is true, but an overriding fact must constantly be borne in mind—that the legal penalty is negligible compared to the penalty imposed by society itself on anyone so exposed. Therefore, it is not only important to change the laws but even more important to change the attitudes of society. This involves changing the public policies of our government regarding federal employment and military services and also our policies regarding the place of the homosexual within the institutional church.

The homosexual and federal employment. John W. Macy, Jr., former chairman of the Civil Service Commission, said, "If an individual applicant were to proclaim publicly that he engages in homosexual conduct, that he prefers such relationships, that he is not sick or emotionally disturbed . . . the Commission would be required to find such an individual unsuitable for federal employment." [10] Mr. Macy went on to say, however, that homosexual tendencies alone are not a sufficient bar to employment. In other words, it's all right to have homosexual tendencies but it isn't all right to exercise them, even in private with consenting adults.

In an elaboration of the major arguments used to ban homosexuals from federal employment, Mr. Macy stated the following:

> Pertinent considerations here are the revulsion of other employees by homosexual conduct and the consequent disruption of service efficiency; the apprehension caused other employees by homosexual advances, solicitations, or assaults; the unavoidable subjection of the sexual deviate to erotic stimulation through on-the-job use of common toilet, shower, and living facilities; the offense to members of the public who are required to deal with known or admitted sexual deviates to transact government business; the hazard that the prestige and authority of a government position will be used to foster homosexual activity, particularly among the youth; and the use of government funds and authority in furtherance of conduct offensive both to the mores and the law of our society.[11]

In this single statement can be found all the examples of the mythology surrounding homosexuality. Virtually every stereotype has been included: the typical homosexual as an effeminate queen swishing around the office making indecent passes at all of the same sex, corrupting youth to the point of assault. To ban all federal employment because of such stereotyping is as unjust as to refuse to hire Negroes because of the stereotype of a Stepin Fetchit. Such a view of the homosexual ignores the truth of the observation made by one of the world's outstanding experts on homosexuality, Dr. D. J. West: "It is now widely accepted that homosexuals may be useful, productive people and not in the least antisocial aside from their sexual peculiarity." [12]

The assumptions made by the Civil Service Commission are based on rigidly held beliefs about homosexuals which describe accurately only a very small percent of the homosexuals in our society, and thus they are all excluded from any kind of employment with the federal government. Other reasons given are that they are emotionally unstable and subject to blackmail. The former raises the whole question of whether or not homosexuals are by definition mentally and/or emotionally ill people. Psychiatrists disagree on this matter. Sigmund Freud, the father of psychoanalysis, wrote the following to an American mother regarding her fears about her son's sexual directions.

> Homosexuality is assuredly no advantage, but it is nothing to be ashamed of, no vice, no degradation—it cannot be classified as an illness; we consider it to be a variation of the sexual function produced by a certain arrest of sexual development. Many highly respectable individuals of ancient and modern times have been homosexuals, several of the greatest men among them (Plato, Michelangelo, Leonardo da Vinci).[13]

The blackmail argument is used not only to ban homosexuals from federal employment but to bar homosexuals from holding security clearances which would enable them to work in private industry having government contracts. The ban on security clearances stems from the 1953 Executive Order defining security risks as sex perverts, heavy drinkers, loose talkers, and persons judged unreliable, untrustworthy, or immoral. Homosexuals are assumed to be emotionally immature, unstable, gossipy, and subject to flattery. That these terms describe some homosexuals is true—just as they also describe many heterosexuals. The major point which is usually forgotten here is that it is the government's attitude toward homosexuality which is the cause of the vulnerability to blackmail. If a homosexual were not in danger of losing his job as a result of exposure, the major reason for fear of being exposed would be eliminated and thus the vulnerability to blackmail would be greatly lessened.

After the unfortunate episode involving Walter Jenkins of President Johnson's staff, the American Mental Health Foundation sent a letter to President Johnson opposing "the kind of hysteria that demands that all homosexual persons be barred from any responsible position." The mere fact that a person is a homosexual does not "per se make him more unstable or more of a security risk than any heterosexual person." In 1955, the Committee on Cooperation with Governmental (Federal) Agencies of the Group for the Advancement of Psychiatry (GAP) made a report on homosexuality in which it noted that it found no evidence to support the assumption that homosexuals are more likely than heterosexuals to submit to the blackmail efforts of foreign agents or more likely to release secrets under the pressure of interrogation.[14]

An interesting case involving the withdrawal of security clearances from a homosexual is that of Benning Wentworth, an electronics technician in a private research laboratory. He held a "secret" security clearance from the Department of Defense for seven years when, in 1966, he was charged with having been involved in homosexual practices with a former air force enlisted man. As a result, his security clearance was revoked. Although he admitted to being a practicing homosexual, he denied the specific charges made against him and challenged the revocation of his security clearance. Mr. Wentworth stated, "My sex life is my own private business. It has no bearing on my job or my loyalty." The defense department claimed that Wentworth's homosexuality made him subject to "coercion, influence, or pressure that may be likely to cause action contrary to the national interest" and therefore he was vulnerable to blackmail which made him a poor security risk. His lawyer pointed out in reply that as an admitted homosexual, he couldn't be blackmailed and that the only pressure and coercion on him was coming from the Department of

Defense. Mr. Wentworth expressed the views of other homosexuals who find themselves discriminated against when he said, "Like anyone else, I want to be judged by my public acts, not my sexual preferences when they harm no one." [15]

The homosexual and military service. The total exclusion of homosexuals from federal employment is extended to all branches of the armed forces, and for approximately the same reasons.

The policy of the defense department is well expressed in a letter from Col. M. P. DiFusco, Assistant Director, Personnel Management, Office of the Assistant Secretary of Defense:

> Department of Defense policy requires prompt separation of a homosexual. The homosexual person is considered unsuitable for military service and is not permitted to serve in the armed forces in any capacity. His presence in a military unit would seriously impair discipline, good order, and the security of the armed forces.
>
> While it is conceivable that homosexual individuals could perform certain military duties in an efficient and acceptable manner, the unique nature of the military environment precludes any possibility of their assimilation within a military organization either as individuals or as a unit. The most obvious of the unique elements in this military environment are communal living conditions, close association on an around-the-clock basis, ashore and at sea, and the necessity for unrestricted assignability of individuals. Others are strict discipline, high unit morale, interdependence of individuals and units, and highest order of security.[16]

The injustice of such a policy is not so much that a whole segment of the population is excluded from military service as that it is a policy which places homosexuals in a hopelessly untenable position. If they admit to their homosexual tendencies, they may not serve but the reason for their not serving could become known and thus jeopardize their entire future, whereas if they deny these tendencies, they will be taken into the armed forces and if exposed will be dismissed with an undesirable discharge which will make them ineligible for any GI benefits plus jeopardizing their future careers.

Obviously, if a homosexual in uniform engages in homosexual acts involving force, fraud, involvement with a minor, or violation of public decency, he should be dismissed—and dishonorably, as would any heterosexual soldier involved in a rape. In the case of a military person who admits to homosexual *tendencies* only or to having participated in homosexual acts prior to military service but who has not been involved in homosexual acts while in service, he is usually given an honorable discharge. Most homosexuals in the military service, however, fall in between the first and last types; that is, those who while in the service have participated in homosexual activities, but with consenting adults in private. Present military policy is to dismiss such persons with an undesirable discharge thus making them ineligible for any GI benefits. It is here that the injustice seems to be most flagrant. If the military believes that such a man is a detriment to the armed forces, he should be permitted to leave without dishonor, assuming his military record is good.

The extent of the injustice which can result from these policies of the armed forces regarding homosexuals is illustrated by Alfred Gross, who has written of what may or may not be an extreme case:

> It is said that when a homosexual is undesirably discharged from the armed forces, the local police are notified. Then he is a marked man in his home community or in whatever place he proposes to settle. . . . One man, who had devoted a lifetime in preparation for a highly specialized craft, found himself unable to work at his trade because many years previously he had told his superiors in the army he was afraid he might get into trouble because of his homosexual tendencies and wanted help. He was discharged without honor within a month. He is still paying for believing an army chaplain's statement: "If anything is troubling you, come and see me about it." [17]

"Church Law" and the Homosexual

What is the attitude of the church that needs rethinking? The church should not exclude homosexuals as a class from membership, ordination, seminaries, or as employees within local parısnes, jurisdictional entities, or in positions of national leadership.

The rationale for this view is based on certain assumptions which I believe to be true as a result of some study of homosexuality:

1. The Christian church has an obligation to accept into its fellowship all who profess the lordship of Jesus Christ. The fact that a man may have homosexual tendencies exercised with consenting adults in private is not an automatic denial of that profession; therefore, it would be a violation of that obligation for the church to deny membership or even leadership to a homosexual on the basis of his homosexuality alone.

2. Much, if not most, of the neuroses identified with homosexuals seems less related to the homosexuality than to the attitude of society toward the homosexual. The British psychiatrist D. J. West spoke to this issue when he said:

> The direction taken by the sexual urge has little relation to abnormal sex traits . . . providing the homosexuals resolve their conflicts by fully and openly accepting their homosexual inclinations. On the other hand, those who remain in the dangerously unstable condition of partially repressed homosexuality are liable to develop all manner of disorders.[18]

Freud, in his letter to the American mother, made a statement which indicates that he believed that homosexuality is not so great a problem as the difficulty of the homosexual to adjust to it. After pointing out that she could not expect treatment to eliminate the homosexual tendencies, he wrote: "What analysis can do for your son runs in a different line. If he is unhappy, neurotic, torn by conflicts, inhibited in his social life, analysis may bring him harmony, peace of mind, full efficiency, whether he remains a homosexual or gets changed." [19] Is it not obvious that the church has a major role to play in helping society understand the nature of homosexuality? It is not possible for the church to meet this responsibility unless it rids itself of its archaic outlook on the homosexual and accepts him into its fellowship and into its employment.

3. The vast majority of homosexuals are not a threat to society

in any way; therefore, policies of exclusion of any kind should be applied to homosexuals on an individual basis and not as a class. Obviously, the fact that some homosexuals may be unable to function effectively as clergymen does not mean that most cannot. In the Kinsey study on sex offenses,[20] fourteen categories of such crimes were cataloged from convictions of 1,356 sex offenders. There were no categories for forced homosexual acts because "cases involving real force in homosexual relations are too infrequent to warrant separate classification." In the case of *People vs. Giani,* the defendant was charged with oral copulation with a fifteen-year-old boy. The district attorney asked the defendant if he was a homosexual. The defendant's lawyer's objection to the question was overruled. On appeal the California Court of Appeals ruled the question invalid and in doing so quoted the California Sexual Deviation Project:

> The facts are that the majority of homosexuals are no particular menace to society. A small number of them, like those who are heterosexual, will attempt to seduce or sexually assault others or try to initiate sex relations with small children. . . . Evidence does not exist for the popular idea that homosexuals are in general antisocial individuals.

4. The assumption is often made that homosexuality is caused by seduction of heterosexuals by homosexuals. This is one of the many myths surrounding homosexuality which has little or no foundation. In their recent book on homosexuality, Peter and Barbara Wyden point out that their extensive study made clear that homosexuals are very rarely interested in children. They write:

> In fact fewer homosexuals than heterosexuals are afflicted with this weakness and even the worst pedophiles are hardly violent types. . . . The experts are unanimous that a reasonably well-adjusted child will automatically and effectively resist advances from adult homosexuals. Even most youngsters who do succumb to seduction do not become homosexuals. . . . In adult seductions, the evidence is equally unanimous. . . . In other words, homosexuals are not pushed into their condition; they can be led, but only if they are ready to walk into it.[21]

The authors also point out that more restrictive laws against homosexuality do not suppress homosexuality, but on the contrary actually tend to encourage it.[22]

5. The assumption of immorality as applied to homosexual acts is at the base of the church's opposition to homosexuals. It is my assumption that sex acts, in themselves, are neither moral nor immoral. Their morality is not in the acts, but in the circumstances wherein the acts take place. When I meet people I judge them by the warmth of their personalities, their attitudes toward others, their character as to honesty, integrity, intelligence. It never occurs to me to be concerned about the manner in which they fulfill their sexual drives. Why shouldn't I judge homosexuals in the same way? I find very persuasive the position taken in November 1967 by ninety Episcopalian priests in their statement that "a homosexual relationship between two consenting adults should be judged by the same criteria as a heterosexual marriage; that is, whether it is intended to foster a permanent relationship of love." [23] The attitude of the Friends in England, I also find wise and mature: "Surely it is the nature and quality of a relationship that matters: one must not judge it by its outward appearance, but by its inner warmth. Homosexual affection can be as selfless as heterosexual affection, and therefore we cannot see that it is some way morally worse." [24]

Apart from the question of whether past treatment and attitudes toward the homosexual have been just, the fact is that relatively recent movements have been taking place among homosexuals and those sympathetic to their cause to bring about the elimination of discriminating practices against homosexuals. This growing militancy among and in behalf of homosexuals has been described in one press report referred to earlier.

Long the target of whispered comments or off-color jokes, homosexuality is fast coming out in the open. Homosexuals in many instances are boldly challenging the right of others to make them second-class citizens. With growing support from heterosexuals, they are fighting discrimination on legal, economic, and social fronts.[25]

There has been a much more lenient attitude toward homosexuals in some areas. Although jobs in the city government of New

York City used to be very difficult to obtain, since the beginning of 1967 the city no longer asks job applicants if they are homosexuals. The New York State Liquor Authority has ruled that state law no longer forbids a bar from serving homosexuals. An increasing number of court cases are being filed in which homosexuals are challenging the laws against their activities, and there seems to be no shortage of non-homosexual lawyers available to defend them. There is also an increasingly greater number of Protestant clergymen coming out publicly in opposition to the laws and government policies against the homosexual.

Many viewers of this trend may conclude that the moral fiber of the nation is in a state of decay, but more objective observers see this as evidence of a more enlightened and mature attitude toward homosexuality—an attitude more in line with that taken by most European nations such as France, England, Belgium, Spain, Greece, Italy, the Netherlands, Denmark, and Sweden. None of these have laws against homosexual practices between consenting adults in private, and in none is the extent of homosexuality any greater than in the United States.

The failure of the law and society to change its attitudes toward the homosexual will perpetuate the second-class citizenship of the typical homosexual who harms no one but finds that this status leaves him vulnerable to all kinds of harassment and extortion, which would not be possible if attitudes were more enlightened. An example of the situation that presently exists is illustrated by the events in an article in a leading newspaper:

> This spring [1966] in New York City local police and FBI agents broke up a 70-man extortion ring that had taken hundreds of thousands of dollars in blackmail money from at least 700 homosexuals throughout the United States. The victims included men from the heights of eminence: two deans of eastern universities, several professors, business executives, a motion picture actor, a television personality, a California physician, a general and an admiral, a member of Congress, a British theatrical producer, and two well-known singers. Another victim, a high-ranking military officer, committed suicide the night before he was to testify to a New York County grand jury investigating the racket.

All were shaken down by crooks posing as police officers

after decoys from the ring got the victims into hotel rooms. In every case the extortionists made the same threats, to expose the homosexuals unless they paid up.[26]

If one can accept the fact that only a very few homosexuals may be a threat to society (as are a few heterosexuals), that the church has a particular obligation to accept all men as children of God and acceptable in his sight, that the major problem facing the homosexual is not his homosexuality but society's attitude toward it, and finally that the nature of the sexual acts between consenting adults in private should not determine whether such people should be permitted into the full life of the church—then what reason is left for the present attitude of the church toward the homosexual? The fact is that homosexuals are in seminaries, they are already within the clergy, and they are holding all sorts of jobs within all levels of the church—and they are doing so competently, efficiently, and to the glory of God.

Therefore, in addition to the other recommendations presented at the beginning of this chapter, the church ought to (1) speak out in support of repeal of laws which make criminal, homosexual practices between consenting adults in private; (2) support a change in the present policies of complete exclusion of homosexuals from federal employment, from induction or enlistment into the armed forces, and from holding security clearances; (3) oppose, where they exist, police policies of enticement and entrapment in the enforcement of laws against solicitation by homosexuals; (4) admit homosexuals, as such, fully into the life and membership of the church; and (5) cease whatever discrimination exists against homosexuals, per se, in admission to seminaries, in ordination, and in employment as national, conference, and local church staff.

the homophile movement

CHAPTER 9

The Homophile Movement in America

FOSTER GUNNISON, JR.

"Equality for Homosexuals" proclaim the red letters emblazoned on white. A youth points with pride to his lapel button. "That's what we're here for," he says.

Seated next to him in the crowded room a second young man sports a different button—"Gay Is Good"—in white on black. What does that mean? "We're all 'gay' here—homosexuals," he explains. "We're fighting for our rights. Here, read this." He hands over a printed sheet of paper.

> Resolved: that this conference, in public affirmation of its belief that homosexuals are in no way inferior to heterosexuals, and that homosexuality is in no way inferior to heterosexuality as a valid way of life, hereby adopt as its official slogan the words "Gay Is Good."

A speaker concludes his spirited oration in favor of the resolution, and takes his seat. The chairman calls for order and then for a vote. All hands shoot into the air. The resolution is adopted.

The conference room is the large main lounge of a gay restaurant in Chicago. It is packed with some seventy men and women of all ages, delegates representing some two dozen homophile[1]

Mr. Foster Gunnison, Jr. is the director of the Institute of Social Ethics, Hartford, Connecticut, which maintains a research library related to the history and development of the homophile movement and its various organizations. Mr. Gunnison is also president of New York's Council on Equality for Homosexuals, and is an official of the North American Conference of Homophile Organizations. He is the author of the booklet *An Introduction to the Homophile Movement*.

organizations spanning the United States and Canada. On request, the chairman of credentials ticks off some of the occupations represented: librarian, biologist, biochemist, secretary, magazine editor, schoolteacher, hotel chef, nurse, shipping clerk, civil engineer, college instructor, insurance salesman.

This is the Fourth Annual Meeting of the North American Conference of Homophile Organizations (NACHO), now entering the final moments of a week-long schedule in August 1968.

Clearly there is an air of militancy here. A committee meeting breaks up and the committee chairman moves to the podium with his report—a resolution that the conference Clearing House send questionnaires to all nine hundred congressional and state gubernatorial candidates in the upcoming November election, requesting their views on matters of discrimination against homosexuals.

What is the Clearing House? "We operate out of Kansas City," explains its director. "We receive publications from each of the organizations and redistribute them to all the organizations along with announcements about NACHO. This way each organization keeps in touch with the others and keeps abreast of developments in the movement. For example, we'll send out this questionnaire to political candidates, tabulate the replies, then mail the results to our organizations."

The candidate-polling proposal is presented and adopted and another speaker heads for the microphone.

"We are proposing the adoption of a Homosexual Bill of Rights," he calls out. Cards are passed out. The cards list five items under "Basic Rights" (e.g., "A person's sexual orientation or practice shall not affect his eligibility for employment with federal, state, or local governments"), plus ten items under "Areas for Immediate Reform" (e.g., "Police shall desist from notifying employers of those arrested for homosexual offenses"). Changes in wording and emphasis are debated by the assembly. A vote is called for, and the Bill of Rights passes unanimously.

The conference chairman, a Protestant minister from the West Coast, calls for the last order of business: where to meet next, in August 1969? Bids go in for several major cities. Houston wins, and the chairman gavels the meeting to a close.

And so, tucked away among the snowballing mass of pressures for social change, one discovers still another disaffected group claiming injustice and demanding reform—a group that has not yet caught the general public's eye, though it appears well on the way to doing so. Relatively few people are aware that there is in this country, and has been for some years, a civil rights movement for homosexuals.

Nor is this a movement of small potential proportions. It is estimated that there are ten to twenty million men and women homosexual citizens in the United States, depending on how much "homosexuality" it takes to be called homosexual. That's enough to populate all of New England and perhaps New York state as well.

Perhaps no other minority group has been as totally misunderstood as it has been totally vilified and rejected. But amid the incredible abundance of myths, half-truths, and cynical speculations that have rendered the subject of homosexuality virtually inaccessible to constructive discourse, there is one thing that stands out as fact. It is that homosexuals, in rapidly increasing numbers, are organizing to challenge a society which would rather pretend they did not exist, and to win for themselves an equal place in that society.

Th struggle began at the close of World War II. Prior to that cataclysmic but catalytic event, the climate of attitude in matters of sex in the United States would hardly have tolerated, much less encouraged, so audacious a frontal attack on prevailing values long held sacrosanct.

The big push came in 1948 with the publication of the first "Kinsey Report," *Sexual Behavior in the Human Male.* The report set everyone on his ear—the homosexual included—with its astonishing facts and figures concerning who, what, and how many, in the realm of sexual deviation.

The report emphasized that homosexuality, like other natural properties, exists as a continuum—a matter not of either/or but of degree; that its incidence was widespread, far beyond what had ever been suspected; and that unorthodox sexual practices were not confined to homosexuals but fully involved heterosexual individuals and married couples as well.

This report, with its huge samples, massive data, meticulous experimental procedures, professional authorship, and affiliation with a major university, plus its unprecedented circulation among the lay public, for the first time put into the hands of the homosexual a potent weapon with which to launch his battle for equality. It also gave him a feeling of moral support that was desperately needed, and a vital, comforting knowledge that he was not alone with his proclivities—either among his own kind or among "normal" people.

Then the cynical sentiments and homosexual-hunting activities of the McCarthy era of the early 1950's had additional galvanizing effect, spurring the formation of homophile organizations and the determination of homosexuals to fight abuses historically submitted to.

In addition, in 1951 there appeared a book by Donald Webster Cory titled *The Homosexual in America: A Subjective Approach.* This was the first comprehensive coverage of the homosexual and his problems by an acknowledged homosexual, and it implied a call to action. The book generated much discussion by homosexuals about what could and should be done, and it helped to reinforce the effort of the Mattachine Foundation—the first major U.S. homophile organization—established around 1950 in Los Angeles.

Initially the Mattachine Foundation was formed as a secret society to promote discussion groups and educational efforts relevant to the subject. At that time homosexuality had hardly achieved the status of a household word, so meetings were held in private homes—behind drawn blinds, with lookouts posted to watch for potential intruders, including police.

Eventually the Foundation went through a reorganization and became the Mattachine Society, Inc. Secrecy was dropped, the effort went "public," and headquarters were shifted to San Francisco.

Prior to this change, some members had broken away to concentrate on publishing materials. This enterprise became One, Inc., of Los Angeles, and it produced a long line of periodicals and other literature. It also won a landmark postal-censorship case at the U.S. Supreme Court level in an effort to get its own publications through the mails. This had the effect of opening the mails to materials from all succeeding homophile organizations. It was a vital contribution to the maintenance of homophile communications both internal and with the public.

Then in 1955 in San Francisco the Daughters of Bilitis was launched, independently of the other two organizations. It was, and still is, the country's only all-female homophile organization.[2]

Together these organizations comprised the pioneering Big

Three of the U.S. homophile movement. One, Inc., and the Daughters are still active in the movement today. The Mattachine Society held similar status until it suffered a decline in the mid-1960's. However, during its heyday it had a number of chapters in other cities around the country. It dropped them all in the early 1960's. A few continued as independents, as "Mattachine" societies or under new names. Thus the original Mattachine operation gave rise to additional organizations around the country.

However, the militancy and eagerness for confrontation evidenced in the recent NACHO meetings and prevalent throughout the movement today, were not characteristic of the organizations of the 1950's. Nor is this surprising. Not only was the homosexual new to his movement, but the forces behind the upheaval in value systems, changing patterns of value support, and general social ferment reflected in events on many fronts today, were only gathering steam then.

Thus the aggressive pursuit of a cause was preceded by a long period of uncertainty and introspection for the homosexual, who had nonetheless taken a major step forward by even joining a homophile organization.

The organizations of the 1950's were preoccupied initially with the *why* of homosexuality. "What are the causes of homosexuality?" members asked themselves and each other. "Why are we this way?" Accordingly much time and effort were expended in poring over material written by psychiatrists and other professionals.

Group discussions and, later, open forums were held to try to search out the answers to these puzzling questions. Guest speakers, authorities of one kind or another, were turned to for definitive answers; but they more often ended up by confusing matters or merely repeating what had already been written. And on occasion they were not above exploiting the situation, aware that a roomful of scared homosexuals made lush hunting grounds for patients, clients, or souls to save. Fortunately these were exceptions.

As time passed and discussions wore on, it became increasingly apparent that indeed there seemed to be no answers. Psychiatrists and others spouted Freud, but Freud himself remained open to question and to interpretation. Ministers quoted the scriptures, but could give no convincing explanation as to why homosexuality was really "bad." And again there was a question of interpretation.

Arguments and explanations of all kinds were closely examined. But in each there seemed something defective—a self-contradiction here, an unsupported assumption there, an arbitrary application of examples or predictions, a surface logic which would not endure searching cross-examination.

Confidence began to grow in the "group" situation which many homosexuals now, for the first time, openly enjoyed. The questioning and counter-questioning became more persistent and more penetrating—and more frustrating until it finally gave way to action.

Action in the 1950's, however, was largely confined to the counseling of homosexuals. There were some efforts toward public education through publications and open discussions. But counseling was the main focus of positive action, and even today most homophile organizations supply counseling services.

Homosexuals in difficulty with the law were referred to sympathetic lawyers. Homosexuals in mental distress were referred to independent-minded psychiatrists or ministers. Homosexuals in need of a job or a place to live were helped to find work and housing. Direct financial assistance was given in some instances.

But little was done to come to grips with the firing personnel manager, the evicting landlord, the reservation-canceling restaurant, the insurance-canceling underwriter, the entrapping policeman, the blackmailing extortionist, the license-revoking alcoholic beverage commission—to say nothing of municipal regulations, state laws, and federal, state, and local official policies and practices that collectively either make the homosexual's life a living hell, or hang like a sword over his head. This was partly a consequence of the scarcity of homophile organizations at the time, and partly of the time itself: it was still next to impossible to find a victimized homosexual willing to press his case or to have it pressed for him.

But picking up the pieces and repairing the damage done to individual homosexuals, worthy an effort though it was, was not destined to carry the movement very far. The wreckage was endless, and the machinery giving rise to it remained untouched.

All this changed with the coming of the 1960's, a decade that seems destined to be remembered for rebellion in many quarters against cumulative social injustice, authoritarian managen-- social and political institutions, and archaic and self-defeating moral codes, with the collective agony of the times a product of past agonies individually borne.

In the case of the homophile movement, additional moral groundwork for change had been laid by the publication in 1955 of a Model Penal Code draft by the American Law Institute, and in 1957 of England's "Wolfenden Report" by the Committee on Homosexual Offenses and Prostitution, both of which constituted recommendations by unimpeachable authorities for legal reform that would have the effect of legitimatizing homosexual relations between consenting adults in private.

Of lesser impact, perhaps, was the adoption in 1961 of the Model Penal Code recommendations by Illinois, the first—and thus far only—state to do so. The "solicitation" statutes, which cause far more grief for homosexuals than the more severely penalized but seldom enforced "sodomy" statutes, remained untouched. (Said one midwestern homophile leader: "We're worse off now than before; now the cops are leaning over backward to get us on 'solicitation' charges.")

The strategic and tactical shifts in the homophile movement, reflecting the increasing openness and militancy of the 1960's, were linked to a succession of key internal events, of which three are noted here. One was a sudden and explosive increase in the number of homophile organizations across the country. The second was the emergence of several pace-setting organizations introducing radical innovations in confrontation, operation, and ideology. The third was the development of collective effort in the form of regional and national networks of homophile organizations.

At the end of 1959 there were fewer than half a dozen organizations in the United States (not counting chapters), and these were headquartered exclusively in the giant coastal cities (mostly the West). By the end of 1965 the number had risen to roughly seventeen (plus chapters), now with increased coverage in the East and Midwest. By the end of 1968 there were nearly forty, including now the South and Southwest, and medium-sized cities such as Hartford, Norfolk, Columbus, and Rock Island.

All this meant a sizable broadening of the base of homophile activity, the nature of which was powerfully influenced by the pace-setting organizations, of which two in particular (one on each coast, east and west) are as noteworthy as they are different from each other.

The Mattachine Society of Washington, D.C. (MSW) sprang up in 1961 as an independent organization unaffiliated with other societies bearing the name Mattachine. (All Mattachine societies are in fact independent of each other today.) In contrast with many of the organizations, it functions as a small, tight, confrontation-minded group, having a membership more oriented than many toward activism. It eschews social activities, preferring to focus primarily on challenging officialdom and secondarily on dispelling prejudice through an active information-education program.

MSW was founded by a physicist-astronomer fired by the U.S. government for homosexuality. Together with his organization, he has developed a clearly formulated, positive ideology, and has injected into the movement a degree of militancy unknown to the previous decade and perhaps undreamed of.

The basic view determining MSW's approach is its hardboiled belief that the progress of the movement now depends less on efforts to enlist, or help, or entertain individual homosexuals, or to explore the "true" nature of homosexuality, than on efforts to smash the discriminatory laws and policies under which homosexuals collectively suffer. And the approach itself, as applied by MSW, pulls no punches.

MSW was, for example, the first homophile organization to adopt a formal statement declaring that homosexuality is neither an illness nor a handicap, and, by implication, criticizing what it viewed as foot-dragging by other organizations preoccupied with promoting "objective" research into homosexuality—a kind of hangover from the 1950's.

But that was only a modest beginning. Washington is the seat of the federal government. The government is seen by the movement as one of the most vicious sources of institutionalized prejudice against the homosexual that exists in this country— worse, for example, than the church or psychiatry, because the consequences are more immediate and the damage done to lives more direct. Not only does the federal government discriminate against homosexuals, but in so doing, it sets a tone for similar discrimination throughout the country by private industry and individuals.

Not only is a homosexual denied employment in civil service jobs, but civil service represents an ever-increasing percentage of *all* jobs. Not only is a homosexual denied security clearance for those jobs in government requiring it, but the denial extends to jobs in private industry doing business with the government under security requirements—again, a growing percentage of *all* jobs.

When a homosexual enlists in or is drafted into the armed forces, he has a choice of declaring himself a homosexual and putting himself on record as such—and the intended confidentiality of these records can be breached in many ways—or failing to declare himself and risking charges of perjury later on. A homosexual already in the service and discovered as such is denied the benefits accruing to veterans and is given a less than honorable discharge which will plague him the rest of his life.

One by one, MSW has tackled these situations head on. The first clash came when a homosexual-baiting congressional subcommittee chaired by Texas representative John Dowdy sought to block MSW's efforts to raise money for its operations by introducing a House bill which would require any organization soliciting funds in the District of Columbia to satisfy the District that all funds collected were destined for "moral" uses.

MSW, ever alert to opportunities for public forums in which to promote its views, eagerly seized the chance to appear on Capitol Hill at the bill's public hearings. It arrived well prepared; it pasted the insulting, insinuating subcommittee, blocked the bill, and stalked out with a carload of publicity.

Then in rapid succession MSW took on the Civil Service Commission and the Department of Defense, in each new case breaking its previous records for imaginativeness and militancy. MSW has, in fact, become the country's leading fount of expertise, in or out of the movement, in the defense of homosexuals victimized by federal government policy—so much so that it is not only regularly consulted by defending attorneys, but itself actually initiates and conducts defenses.

Developing the crucial position that one's sexual orientation per se is irrelevant to the quality of one's performance in a job, MSW moved to extract from the Civil Service Commission the precise reasons for its refusal to employ or retain homosexuals. The Commission not only refused to give reasons but also refused repeated requests to meet with MSW representatives to discuss its anti-homosexual policies. So after several warnings that brought no response, MSW inaugurated the "homophile picket," complete with signs, leaflets, and strict rules emphasizing decorum and good appearance; and twenty-five brave souls marched in front of the Commission building in downtown Washington, and were watched in open-mouthed disbelief by hundreds of passersby.

Shortly thereafter, the Commission acceded to meeting with MSW representatives, requested a formal statement of MSW's views, and responded with a letter detailing its reasons.[3] Pathetic in logic though the reasons seemed, the letter nonetheless marked the first time the Commission had been forced to spell them out, thus opening the door to further attacks by MSW.

MSW's introduction of the picket was at the time viewed with alarm by many other homophile organizations still somewhat chilly in the feet, but now the picket is generally accepted across the country as a sometimes useful tactic for the movement. Subsequent pickets, relevant to particular issues, were staged by MSW in concert with other organizations at the White House, the Pentagon, the State Department, and Independence Hall in Philadelphia. The Independence Hall demonstration has, in fact, become an annual occasion, every Fourth of July, as a general protest symbol, with most eastern organizations participating.

With respect to the Department of Defense, MSW's attacks have had a twofold effect: (1) exposing the basic illogic entailed in the Department's refusal to grant homosexuals security clearances, and (2) exposing the high-handedness with which departmental investigative and hearing proceedings are conducted.

Here the press conference has proved an invaluable tool. The Department of Defense has developed its anti-homosexual policies primarily on the assumption that homosexuals fear exposure and are therefore prime targets for blackmail. Rather than waste time arguing whether homosexuals are in fact coerced into divulging classified information (the record indicates not), MSW takes the forthright approach of having its defendants publicly announce their homosexuality—thus nullifying the blackmail argument—and calls a press conference for the occasion, sometimes in the corridors of the Pentagon itself. The press not only witnesses the declaration but is treated to an exposé of the Department's proceedings, with emphasis on their shortcomings in terms of normal due process as well as on the prevailing vicious circle wherein the Department's own rules and regulations create the very threat of blackmail the government presumes to guard against.

MSW has also gone after the armed forces, most recently as consultants to groups of WACs in two different parts of the country who are threatened with discharges for homosexuality. MSW advises on tactics and strategy, and in one of the cases has also written letters to the army threatening to publicize the witch-hunt and has supplied copies of the leaflet "How to Handle a Federal Interrogation" to aid the servicewomen in their fight.

Thus has MSW in its running battles with the U.S. government set a new pace and established new directions and developed new tactics for the homophile movement.

But militancy can also be effectively expressed in other ways.

One of the greatest problems—if indeed not *the* greatest problem—for the homosexual in his struggle for equality is that not only is he coerced and shamed into hiding, but that he *can* hide. Lacking visible identification, the homosexual, to borrow a phrase from another movement, too easily "passes for white."

"Until we are willing to speak out openly and frankly in defense of our activities, and to identify ourselves with the millions pursuing these activities," wrote Cory, "we are unlikely to find the attitudes of the world undergoing any significant change." [4] Many homophile leaders of today would agree.

The problem is to get the homosexual into public view so that he can be put to work fighting for his rights and the public can see him as the normal, useful person that he really is. But many homosexuals would have neither the interest nor the courage to ally themselves with, nor would they by temperament fit in with, a business-only civil rights organization like MSW. But they *would* associate themselves with an organization like San Francisco's Society for Individual Rights (SIR). And indeed they did.

SIR was founded in 1964 by homosexuals who were dissatisfied with the then sluggish condition of the movement in San Francisco and were chafing at the bit to get moving on a high-powered social program to involve as many of their city's gay community as possible.

In an incredibly short time they put together a social organization the size and scope of which have not been approached in the history of the movement. They set up temporary quarters in an outlying part of the city. With a virtually unrestricted admissions policy they piled up a huge membership. After a few skirmishes with the police and public officials, they succeeded in putting an end to some of the more flagrant forms of abuse and harassment of homosexuals in San Francisco. They scheduled countless dances, buffets, outings, and other social affairs, and operated their own thrift shop. With revenues from these activities they bought their own building right in the heart of downtown San Francisco in full view of the public, and converted it into a full-blown community center for homosexuals complete with offices, dance floor, stage, activity rooms, and food facilities.

In no time they had a full program of planned social-recreational-cultural events scheduled for every day of the week, plus major special functions scattered throughout the year.

But SIR did not limit itself solely to the social sphere, though that has always remained a basic focus of interest. It has, in concert with other San Francisco organizations, assisted in the establishment and/or maintenance of additional local homophile organizations of varying types, such as the (equally pace-setting) Council on Religion and the Homosexual, the Tavern Guild (a first-of-its-kind protective association for gay bars and restaurants), and the National Legal Defense Fund (for selective support of homophile test cases).

It has, again in concert with other organizations, engaged in—and sometimes pioneered—a variety of cause-oriented confrontation tactics, from picketing (e.g., San Francisco's Federal Building on the employment issue) to outright political campaigning (e.g., SIR's famous "Candidates' Night" held before local elections, in which all candidates for office are invited to appear at SIR's community center to express their views on various homophile issues, these views being then communicated to the city's entire homosexual community in conjunction with a voter registration drive).

In short, SIR has become a well-rounded, well-run organization, a model for popular grassroots support at the local level, as MSW has become a model for national battlefront action.

But SIR and MSW, models though they be, are not the only exponents of the new militancy of the 1960's.

Today, for example, on the ground that homosexuals know as much about homosexuals as anyone else, and probably more, homophile organizations everywhere are demanding whenever meetings, public or private, are held to discuss homosexuality, that homophile representatives be included among the speakers or participants. Thus, in spring 1968, the Student Homophile League (SHL), headquartered at Columbia University, picketed to protest a symposium scheduled by Columbia's College of Physicians and Surgeons for medical students. The topic was homosexuality, and not only had SHL been refused any representation on the panel of "experts" (various professionals, four out of five of whom were decidedly anti-homophile in their views) but SHL members were denied admission to the audience (reportedly out of fear that they would challenge the panelists).

Homophile organizations are also demanding an end to a variety of discriminatory policies and harassment practices at local levels. Thus in 1966 the Mattachine Society of New York (widely noted for its aggressive protection of the city's homosexuals through direct contacts with top city officials) staged a successful "sip-in" to challenge regulations affecting homosexuals' right to drink in public establishments.

In similar fashion organizations across the country [5] are striking out in imaginative ways to educate the public and the professions, and bring pressure to bear on the principal sources of governmental, industrial, and private discrimination against the homosexual.

However, until a few years ago, the country's homophile organizations generally operated alone in their respective cities or territories, with little inter-organizational effort.

There had been some exceptions at local or regional levels. Cooperation among the San Francisco organizations and—in picketing projects—the eastern organizations has already been mentioned. Similarly, groups in the Los Angeles area have worked together on certain projects. Also, several court cases around the country—on censorship, bar license revocation, civil service employment, etc.—have at one time or another attracted the mutual support of geographically disparate organizations. But none of these efforts represented either formal association or national scope.

Perhaps the closest thing to a formal regional association was East Coast Homophile Organizations (ECHO), formed in 1963. After three annual conferences (in Philadelphia, Washington, and

New York, respectively) the association became inactive, but not before it had given birth, unintentionally, to a far grander effort.

It was in the fall of 1965, near the close of the final ECHO conference in New York, that a special private meeting of east coast and other (visiting) homophile leaders was held to see what might be done to promote interorganizational cooperation around the country. They decided to call another meeting with broader representation from far-flung organizations to discuss the matter further. But it was apparent that the idea of a truly national network of homophile organizations had begun to take firm hold in the minds of some.

And so, four months later, in February 1966, forty delegates from fourteen organizations—the most prominent of the country's homophile leaders—met for a weekend at a hotel in Kansas City. This was to become the first in the current series of NACHO conferences. And it was here that groundwork was laid for moving in the direction of a formal, if loosely structured, national affiliation.

Six months later, in August, twenty-four organizations sent sixty delegates to a meeting at a hotel in downtown San Francisco. And the following year a third conference with much the same representation was held at no less a prestigious place than George Washington University in Washington, D.C. The next, and most recent, conference was held in August 1968 in Chicago (see opening of this chapter).

At these meetings, position statements were adopted (e.g., a declaration that homosexuality is neither sickness nor handicap). Press conferences and local radio and TV interviews were held. Administrative committees were established, and project committees were formed to deal with armed forces discrimination, law reform, new organizations, movement unity, research, and political tactics.

Conference administrative machinery was installed, including executive officers and a governing council. And regional conferences of homophile organizations—east, midwest, and west—were established to take up matters of regional concern, and to promote liaison and maintain continuity of effort between annual national conferences.

It should be noted that around the time NACHO was taking shape, events were occurring outside the movement which provided additional moral support. Among these were the publication of *Towards a Quaker View of Sex* (1963, 1964) by a group of British Friends, *Time for Consent* (1967) by British theologian Norman Pittenger, and the new *Dutch Catechism* (1967), all of which represented major strides in religious reevaluations of homosexuality.

In the area of law, a notable victory was the final adoption in 1967 by Parliament of the Wolfenden Committee's recommendations, so that private consensual adult homosexual relations are no longer a crime in Great Britain. And in countries which have long been free of such legal strictures, there are reports (Denmark) of progress on such finer points as joint filing of income tax for homosexual couples who have remained together for several years.

At home, in 1968 the renowned research psychologist Evelyn Hooker was appointed chairman of a special nationwide study committee on homosexuality sponsored by the National Institute of Mental Health. Dr. Hooker is prominent in a growing line of contemporary professional researchers whose collective findings suggesting homosexuals to be neither sick nor different are putting to shame the shabby studies and banal opinions of well-meaning clinical practitioners and professors of psychiatry for whom sound scientific research remained only an aspiration.

These and similar events have contributed to the rising confidence of American homosexuals, and the new militancy of their movement.

Not rehabilitation, not cure, not acceptance of homosexuals as "persons" in distinction from their "acts," not restriction of their acts to a special privacy out of sight and out of mind—none of these is remotely part of the ideologies and programs now developing in the movement. To the organized homosexual such aims are perverted, such distinctions false. And all are flatly rejected along with institutions and professions proposing them. The old question of the 1950's, "Why are we what we are?" has given way to the statement, "Here we are, regardless of how or why we got here; now let's take it from there."

Significantly, the 1967 NACHO conference adopted as part of its Credentials Program—by which organizations are accredited for admission and participation—several standards for organizational aims and purposes, including "the establishment in society of the homosexual as a first-class citizen and a first-class human being" and "the unqualified acceptance by society of homosexuality as a mode of self-expression no less valued than heterosexuality."

And the following year the conference adopted the slogan "Gay Is Good," reported at the beginning of this chapter.

In short, the homosexual wants to be accepted by society—not in spite of his homosexuality, but together with it. And he wants himself *and* his homosexuality, and other homosexuals and *their* homosexuality, not merely to be tolerated, but to be positively valued as worthy contributors to the social order and as a worthy way of life; to be positively valued as a symbol, perhaps, of the uniqueness and variety of feeling and experience which set man apart from other life; as a symbol, perhaps, that society, whatever else its faults, sets no cruel barriers to the expression of human love.

CHAPTER 10

Gay Is Good

FRANKLIN E. KAMENY

More, probably, than any other significant sociological phenomenon in our society, homosexuality remains immersed in a sea of persistent misimpressions, myths, folklore, and legends.

In significant part, this arises because the subject is usually discussed by people who are only onlookers with a sketchy knowledge and an often-biased viewpoint based upon highly nonrepresentative samplings of the group of which they speak, and from which samplings they then make improper and unwarranted generalizations—people like clergymen, psychiatrists and psychoanalysts, doctors, lawyers, policemen, and those in various social and counseling services, whose sampling is preselected for a high incidence of emotional and social maladjustment and problems.

As a result, discussions of homosexuality tend to sink quickly into a morass of psychiatry, criminal law, moral theology, emotional disturbance, "abnormality," "deviance," and the like, most if not all of which is irrelevant or only peripherally relevant to the average, ordinary, guilt-free, unanguished, reasonably untroubled, basically happy homosexual, whose major problems in regard to his homosexuality are not emotional problems but much more likely to be employment problems not of his own making.

Dr. Franklin E. Kameny is an astronomer and physicist, with a Ph.D. from Harvard University. He is founder and president of the Mattachine Society of Washington (D.C.); cochairman of the Washington Area Council on Religion and the Homosexual; chairman of the Eastern Regional Conference of Homophile Organizations; chairman of the Committee on the Federal Government, of the North American Conference of Homophile Organizations. Dr. Kameny has acted as personal counsel in a number of federal government security clearance, civil service employment, and military cases involving homosexuals or allegations of homosexuality.

Such discussions, too, are always saturated with a pervasive, pernicious, insidious—and deeply destructive—negativism, often quite unrecognized as such, which literally saturates every approach to the matter and colors initial assumptions and approaches, logic and reasoning, and final conclusions. This negativism is based upon unquestioned assumptions that homosexuality is undesirable, or less desirable than heterosexuality; that it is inferior to heterosexuality; that it is a second-rate condition, to be put up with at worst, and to be changed at best.

Increasingly, homosexuals are becoming impatient with the place of their traditional role as that of a mere passive, silent battlefield, across which conflicting "authorities" parade and fight out their questionable views, prejudices, and theories. Increasingly, homosexuals are insisting upon a role in which they are not seen as mere specimens to be examined and discussed, but as active, informed participants in the consideration of their condition and in the disposition of their fate.

This short essay will be an attempt to discuss a few aspects of homosexuality from the viewpoint of one of those most concerned, most knowledgeable and, unfortunately, least consulted—the homosexuals themselves.[1]

Therefore the approach taken here will be a positive one: that homosexuality is not an inferior state; that it is neither an affliction to be cured nor a weakness to be resisted; that it is not less desirable for the homosexual than heterosexuality is for the heterosexual; that the homosexual is a first-class human being and first-class citizen, entitled, by right, to all of the privileges and prerogatives of his citizenship, and to all of the God-given dignity of his humanity—as the homosexual that he is and has a moral right to continue to be; that homosexuality is nothing to be ashamed of, nothing to be apologetic about, nothing to bemoan, but something around which the homosexual can and should build part of a rewarding and productive life and something which he can and should enjoy to its fullest, just as heterosexuality is for the heterosexual.

We might commence with some examples of the negativism mentioned, with commentary where appropriate. A full listing would be almost endless; a few illustrations will suffice to indicate the pattern.

The overt negativism of the a priori, untested assumption, by psychoanalysts—used as their conceptual starting point—that all adult homosexuality is pathological.[2]

The widely touted assertion that homosexuality is indicative of immaturity. This arises, in part, from a misinterpretation by Freud and others, of a cultural artifact growing out of the barriers placed, in past years, in the way of comfortable relationships between young people of both genders, and in part upon circular reasoning which unwarrantedly uses heterosexuality as part of the definition of maturity. The negative effects of this unfounded assertion of immaturity are insidious, pernicious, and extensive, in terms both of general attitudes toward the homosexual and of the homosexual's self-image.

The condemnation of certain family patterns, not because they are intrinsically bad, but because—supposedly—they produce homosexual children. Thus although there is no actual evidence which will withstand careful examination, the very widespread, widely accepted assertion that the pattern of a strong, dominant, affectionate mother, and a submissive, distant father produces homosexuals is used as a basis for condemnation of this harmless, very common departure from the traditional familial mold.

The almost universal characterization of homosexuality as something purely physical and lustful, devoid of elements of love and affection. In our anti-sexual society, this is a particularly strong condemnation. So deep lying is this concept of homosexuality that a supposedly authoritative psychoanalyst of some note said, "The idea may be at least theoretically entertained that a homosexual adult love relationship can exist." [3] For the many homosexual couples living in lasting, stable, mature, deeply affectionate love relationships, such a statement is patronizing and offensive (and somewhat ludicrous), and is indicative of the shallow, misinformed approach commonly found. In point of fact, homosexuality is far more a matter of love and affection than it is commonly considered to be; and heterosexuality is far more a matter of physical lust than our culture, with its over-romanticized approach, admits it to be. Actually, homosexuality and heterosexuality differ but little, if at all, in this respect.

The almost universal tendency, in consideration of the possible nature of and origins of homosexuality, to examine a variety of "problems" or pathological alternatives—defective family background, glandular imbalance, etc.—but never even to consider the possibility that homosexuality is nothing other than a non-pathological preference, not different in kind or origins from heterosexuality. Obviously, if no non-pathological alternatives are even considered, homosexuality *will* be found to be pathological, or to result from a disturbed or defective background.

The rather patronizing attitude, often expressed by the most well-meaning and seemingly enlightened, which says something to the effect that "these poor, afflicted people should not be punished for the weakness from which they suffer." But of course, as indicated elsewhere, homosexuality is no affliction, no weakness, and nothing being suffered from.

The attitude of many that the way to improve the status of the homosexual is through "reform" of the homosexual. One does not eliminate irrational and unfounded prejudice by reforming the victims of that prejudice; one reforms the prejudiced. Many of these same people, while piously disclaiming any desire to change the practice of homosexuals to heterosexuality, will subscribe, in the name of freedom of choice, to the idea that "of course those who *wish* to change should be assisted to do so," without realizing that the majority of those who wish to change are doing so in surrender to the prejudice around them (quite as much as are those Negroes who try to "pass" as white) either because life has been made uncomfortable for them or because they have been persuaded ("brainwashed" might be a better word) into a false feeling that they and their homosexuality are inferior to heterosexuals and heterosexuality. The immorality of surrender to prejudice ranks second only to the immorality of prejudice itself.

The nonobjective terminology, saturated with subjective, negative value judgments, used with great frequency by the medical profession in discussing treatment of homosexuals, in which change from homosexuality to or toward heterosexuality is characterized as "improvement," "recovery," "successful" therapy, etc. The homosexual is considered "helped" not by assistance in adjustment to his homosexuality—probably the only legitimate goal, when therapy is needed—but by the extent to which he is enabled—or pressured—into entering into heterosexual relationships.

The oft-repeated statement that "of course" all homosexuals would convert to heterosexuality if only they could. Quite aside from the factual inaccuracy of the statement—surveys have shown that most homosexuals would not change—never do we see anyone coming to grips with the basic question of *why* the homosexual should change to heterosexuality, even if he could. Obviously, if the disadvantages, disabilities, and penalties which the homosexual faces are a result of society's prejudices—and of course they are, in their entirety—then suggesting that the homosexual improve his lot by submission to those prejudices, at cost of his personal integrity, is fundamentally immoral. One does not propose to solve the problems of anti-Semitism by conversion of Jews to Christianity, much as that might improve the life of many individual Jews. The homosexual has a right to remain a homosexual, and in fact, a moral obligation to do so, in order to resist immoral prejudice and discrimination, no matter how possible, practical, and easy a change to heterosexuality might be.

The endlessly reiterated theme of psychiatrists, psychoanalysts, and others that homosexuality is a fear of relating to, and an inability to relate to, members of the opposite sex, or a fear of women. This is no more true, of course, than to say that *hetero*sexuality arises from fear of relating to, or an inability to relate to, members of the same sex, or a fear of men. (Both are true in some instances, of course.) This theme makes of homosexuality something negative, whereas, as the majority of homosexuals are very well aware, homosexuality is as positive an attraction toward members of the same sex as heterosexuality is toward those of the opposite sex.

The casual use of terms such as "queer" by sensitive people of a liberal turn of mind, who would never think of using equivalent, no more offensive terms such as "nigger," "kike," "wop," etc. It is quite clear that whatever the users of those terms may claim on an intellectual basis, they are quite willing, at an emotional level, to deal with homosexuals as something less than full human beings with the same right to human dignity as others.

Application of the pejorative term compulsive to a strong, continuing, or exclusive preference for homosexual relationships, when the same term is not applied to identical preferences for heterosexual relationships. The statement is usually made that persistence in such a preference despite strong societal disapproval and sanctions must indicate pathology. The invalidity of such reasoning can be seen easily enough by applying it to the case of Jews in an anti-Semitic context, or Protestants or Catholics or others in any of the many countries or societies intolerant of their religious persuasion. Obviously an individual does not have to be compulsive or otherwise pathological in order to persist in refusing to subordinate his own individuality to societal conformity.

Statements frequently made, alleging—incorrectly—an increase in the incidence of homosexuality. Rarely are these phrased objectively. Almost always we see such negative phrases as "an *alarming* increase in homosexuality."

The much more subtle negativism seen in "assurances" by well-meaning people that changing the law to legalize private, adult, homosexual acts is not going to lead to an increase in homosexuality—with the obvious implication that "of course" homosexuality is undesirable and that, therefore, while we should not make criminals out of homosexuals, we should not do anything which might increase their number.

The incredible callousness and blunted sensitivity of others who cavalierly dismiss homosexuals from full membership in the human race by saying—falsely, as it turns out, and with an utter disregard for the effects of arrest and imprisonment upon people —that the criminal laws against certain private, adult, consensual homosexual acts must be maintained to provide an incentive for change to heterosexuality. At the very least, there seems to be a severe loss of both perspective and sense of proportion here.

Sex education classes in the schools in which homosexuality is almost universally portrayed as something undesirable, and the homosexual as someone to be shunned. Few people planning such courses, with an exaggerated and ill-conceived regard for what they consider to be the welfare of heterosexual students, ever stop to consider what they are doing to the students in those classes who are homosexuals and who are listening to themselves being described as unacceptable, less-than-human lepers. Apparently the psychological welfare of homosexual students is not important.

The attitudes and policies of our federal government which, by attempted exclusion of homosexuals from civil service employment, from eligibility for security clearances and for inclusion in the armed services (quite ineffectively, let it be said; the actual percentage of homosexuals in each of the three areas is not significantly different from the percentage in the populace at large) upon grounds which, when examined beneath the sometimes superficially persuasive legalistic verbiage with which they are disguised, are seen to be little more than concessions to the unpopularity of homosexuals. Unfortunately, federal policies set the tone and tenor for attitudes and policies on the part of private employers and private citizens generally. Consequently, had the homosexual the visibility of the Negro, there would be some fifteen million unemployed homosexuals in America. One effect of these governmental policies is the surrounding of homosexuals, in the minds of the larger community, with an aura of unreliability, irresponsibility, and disloyalty, quite unwarranted by facts.

Endless theorizing about the causes of homosexuality. While objective inquiry into the causes of homosexuality and the processes leading to it may be a valid scientific exercise of minor intellectual value or importance, the inquiries *actually* made are not at all objective. It quickly becomes apparent that what is being asked is *not* the objective "What causes homosexuality?" but "What goes wrong to cause homosexuality?" or "What can be done to prevent homosexuality?" or "What can be done to change homosexuals into heterosexuals?" These are clearly non-objective questions, laden with a negative value judgment upon homosexuality. There is exactly as much reason, but no more, to inquire about the causes of *homo*sexuality as there is to inquire about the causes of *hetero*sexuality. Yet we see no inquiries made as to what family environment causes a heterosexual to become so; as to what relationships among father, mother, and child lead to heterosexuality, etc. These are equally valid questions of no lesser importance. They are rarely, if ever, asked. We will never learn what causes homosexuality until we have found a valid answer to the question What causes heterosexuality? or What are the processes through which a person becomes a heterosexual? No one even bothers to ask these questions.

Like members of other minority groups, homosexuals are interested in their rights, freedom, and basic human dignity, as homosexuals, and are little if at all properly concerned with how they got to be that way. We did not see the late Dr. Martin Luther King devoting much of his attention to futile debates about which gene on which chromosome causes a black skin. There is no more reason for debates with respect to the cause of homosexuality.

The universal "raising of hackles" at any slightest suggestion or imputation of so-called proselytism on behalf of homosexuality. It must be kept in mind that the homosexual has long been the object of one of the most intensive, evangelical, crusading efforts at proselytism that history has ever seen, directed at converting him to heterosexuality. In fairness, one would expect that what is sauce for the goose would be sauce for the gander. In actual fact, of course, the whole question is academic, since changes but very rarely, if ever, occur in either direction.

The portrayals of homosexuals and homosexuality in current movies. Rarely if ever do we see homosexuals shown as sensitive, admirable, affectionate, likable human beings, and homosexuality as something enjoyable, satisfying, and rewarding, and as an expression of love and affection. Homosexuals are far from perfect, and homosexuality is certainly not all sweetness, love, and light; but of course exactly the same is true, in precisely equal measure, of heterosexuals and heterosexuality. But we see all sides and aspects of heterosexuality portrayed. We see only caricatures, portraying the sordid, the sad, the unpleasant, and the ridiculous—the negative—side of homosexuality.

Finally, the contempt, ridicule, derision, scorn, despisal, denigration, and belittlement of himself and of his condition, the assault upon his right to his very existence as a homosexual, which the homosexual faces at every turn, continuingly and everywhere, often vicious, totally non-supportive, totally unrelieved, except within his own community.

It is possible to go on citing such examples at considerably greater length, but the point has been made clearly. The homosexual is faced at every turn with a relentless barrage of assaults upon his self-esteem and his dignity. While any one of the items listed, taken by itself, might be considered small, trivial, and insignificant, when taken together they add up to a concentrated and rather virulent dose of psychological poison. It is certainly not unexpected, therefore, that many homosexuals suffer from damaged self-image, lack of self-confidence, diminished self-esteem, unwillingness to come forward as homosexuals.

A rereading of the examples cited above will show that a significant number flow from the basic attitude of the medical profession—particularly psychiatry and psychoanalysis—that homosexuality is a sickness or disorder, or a symptom of a sickness or disorder. This essay is neither the place for an extended exposition of the pros and cons of theories alleging the pathology of homosexuality nor for an exploration in depth of the grave failings of medicine, psychiatry, and psychoanalysis vis-à-vis homosexuality. Suffice it to say that the intellectual burden of an adequate demonstration of the pathology of homosexuality obviously rests upon those making the allegations of pathology, and that they have not shouldered their burden.

In past years, that which was considered objectionable was condemned by the "high priests" as sinful. Later, the lawyers took over, and the key to condemnation became criminality. Nowadays, sin is not fashionable anymore, and the criminal law on sexual matters is held in disrepute and is well-nigh universally disregarded; so our latter-day high priests, the psychiatrists and psychoanalysts, perpetuate the traditional condemnation by terming homosexuality a sickness. The basis for the designation in all three contexts is neither fact nor logic, but a subjective negative attitude—prejudice, in short—often well concealed, but no less discreditable for being classified under morality or law, or being misclassified under science.

An examination of the extensive professional literature upon homosexuality shows that the conclusion that homosexuality is a sickness founders upon three major bases, which should be considered very briefly in order to dispose of the entire theory.

First, we find slovenly definitions of terms such as pathology, sickness, neurosis, disturbance, etc. When any effort is made to define these terms, the definitions usually amount to little more than mere nonconformity. As discussed above, if the individual persists in his nonconformity, his actions are then *compulsive*— one of the psychiatrists' "dirty words," saved for the ultimate in condemnation.

Second, and most important, we find a total failure to attend properly to even the most elementary and basic techniques of experimental and observational science. In particular, we see massive tomes written and extensive "research" projects undertaken, based completely upon patients who have come to a psychiatrist's office, and totally without the use of control groups so basic to the validity of any scientific investigation. One can imagine the judgments as to the psychic health of the *hetero*sexual population which would be drawn by a psychiatrist who, through some strange set of circumstances, saw only those heterosexuals who came to him as patients.

Third, we find assumptions of pathology inserted at the outset, only to be drawn out as conclusions. One of the more flagrant examples of this was quoted near the beginning of this chapter.

Basically, what we find is an almost unparalleled example of shoddy, slovenly, slipshod, just plain bad science—and that is said with no little indignation and sense of offense by this author as a scientist by profession, training, and background. In short, homosexuality has been *defined* into sickness by subjective, personal, social, moral, cultural, and religious value judgments, cloaked and camouflaged in the language of science. Therefore, *in the continuing absence of valid scientific evidence to the contrary, homosexuality per se cannot properly be considered a sickness, illness, disturbance, disorder, or pathology of any kind, nor a symptom of any of these, but must be considered as a preference, orientation, or propensity, not different in kind from heterosexuality, and fully on par with it.*

With this whole matter of sickness out of the way, it is possible to take consideration of the entire subject off the psychoanalyst's couch and out of the psychiatrist's office, and to place it into proper perspective so it can be dealt with constructively.

Thus homosexuality is not a psychiatric or medical problem in emotional disturbance or disorder, and psychiatrists, psychoanalysts, and doctors are not the authorities on the subject; it is a *sociological* problem in entrenched prejudice and discrimination directed against a minority group.

In their entirety, the problems of the homosexual as such are—or stem directly from—problems of prejudice and discrimination directed against this minority by the hostile majority around them.

It has been said that there is no Negro problem, that there is really a white problem. It can as accurately be said that there is no homosexual problem, that there is really a heterosexual problem.

It will stand repetition to note that despite common misconceptions, the average homosexual is a reasonably well-adjusted, reasonably happy person, whose problems, if he has any at all in regard to his homosexuality, are much more likely to be employment problems than emotional problems. Medicine, psychiatry, psychoanalysis, etc., are as irrelevant to a constructive consideration of the problems of the average homosexual or to dealing with homosexuality itself, as they are to a parallel consideration of the problems of the average heterosexual, or to dealing with heterosexuality itself.

Once the sickness fantasy has been disposed of, it is possible to draw the necessary parallels to demonstrate that homosexuals are simply another of the minority groups which make up our nation, not different, as such, from religious, ethnic, so-called racial, and other minorities, with problems best appreciated and solved along exactly the same lines as the problems of those other minorities—by seeking to change attitudes and practices *not* of the minority itself, but of those of the majority who discriminate in word and in deed. After all, there is very little fundamental difference in basic essence between the corporation which will not hire Jews or Negroes, and the U.S. Civil Service Commission which will not hire homosexuals.

This classification of homosexuals as a minority group is one which is often met with singular resistance, upon rather specious grounds. Since it is basic to a positive and constructive approach to the question, it is not out of order to explore it briefly.

When we examine the groups which we consider as minorities, we find a thoroughly mixed bag, seeming upon first impression to have nothing in common: Jews and Catholics; Italians, Irish, and Poles; Negroes, Chinese, and Indians; etc. With considerable justification, as will be seen shortly, we may even class women as a minority group, although they hold a numerical majority. What do all of these groups, in terms of their minority status, have in common? Upon examination, we find four characteristics which can be used to define a sociological minority group.

1. A defining characteristic or set of closely related characteristics. This can be skin color, mode of religious observance, country of ancestral origin, gender, etc. The characteristic can be inherent or inborn (e.g., skin color or gender) or environmentally determined (e.g., religion). It can be unalterable (e.g., skin color) or alterable (e.g., religion). Its origin and permanence are not of importance. What is important is how the larger society responds or reacts to it.

2. Prejudice and discrimination. Because of the defining characteristic, but not in logical consequences of it, members of the minority group are subjected to adverse prejudice and discrimination. Because, for example, of the color of a Negro's skin, but not in logical consequence of it, he is made the object of adverse prejudice and discrimination.

3. Depersonalization, dehumanization, stereotyping, group culpability. Let a white, Anglo-Saxon, heterosexual Protestant commit a crime, make himself offensive, or make himself foolish, and he alone, personally and individually, bears the consequences of his actions. Let a member of a minority group do the same, and the culpability is generalized to "all Negroes are . . . ," "all Jews are . . . ," etc. Stereotypes are formed, and the member of the minority is not judged and dealt with as an individual upon his own merits and demerits, strengths and weaknesses, but as a stereotype that has no relationship to more than a very small number of the real people involved. (Very few Negroes are stupid, dirty, and lazy; very few Jews have certain objectionable personality traits; very few homosexuals are effeminate. There are whites, Christians, and heterosexuals who have all of those traits.)

Thus there develops a process of depersonalization and dehumanization which is part of the minority condition.

4. Internalization, group identity. In response to the attitudes and actions of the surrounding majority, the minority group internalizes its feelings. There develop attitudes of "we" and "they," ingroups, subcultures, "ghettos," etc. The minority characteristic becomes the very definition of the person, both in his own eyes and in those of the majority. There are few characteristics of a man which are of lesser importance than the color of his skin. Yet the Negro looks upon himself first as a black—and only later in terms of the truly significant and meaningful facets of his being. This, of course, is part of the human breakage caused by the minority condition.

Even casual consideration will show that all of the diverse and disparate groups which we consider as sociological minority groups meet the four criteria just set forth. Consideration will show that the homosexual also meets these criteria. Thus once homosexuality has been removed from the category of a pathological state it can be brought into company with other minority conditions, and need not stand out as something warranting totally unique treatment, but as merely one more problem in irrational and immoral prejudice.

The effects upon the homosexual of the kind of unmitigated, unrelenting negativism discussed are severe. As stated, they include damaged self-image, lowered self-esteem, doubts and uncertainties as to personal worth, an attitude of self-deprecation, and a false and unwarranted sense of an inferiority and undesirability of the homosexual condition—in short, all the complex forms of damage to personality which accompany membership in a minority.

For many years, and continuingly, the effect of these attitudes resulted in an almost universal covertness and secrecy upon the part of homosexuals. More recently, however, there has developed a growing militancy and rebellion by homosexuals against the position into which they are placed.

There has always been a minority of homosexuals—far fewer than commonly believed—who desired to convert to heterosexuality, if possible. It has been pointed out that this desire is, of course, the consequence of the same kind of brainwashing which has resulted in the efforts by many Negroes to "pass" as white;

the related usage, by many, of hair-straightening devices; etc. The response by the Negro is understandable in a society in which black is equated with all that is bad, evil, immoral, undesirable, dirty, and ugly, and white with all that is good, pure, moral, desirable, clean, and beautiful. In an effort to counter these feelings, the Negro community has had some measure of success through the adoption of the slogan "Black is beautiful."

In a parallel effort to replace negative feelings upon the part of the homosexual—or at the least, a kind of grudging, wishy-washy acceptance of his homosexuality as something that perhaps is not so bad, if nothing better is possible—with the positive feelings of pride, self-esteem, self-confidence, and self-worth so necessary to true human dignity, the North American Conference of Homophile Organizations (at the suggestion of this writer) has adopted the slogan which is the theme of this essay: "Gay is good."

"Good" has a number of meanings. Homosexuality is good in terms of all of them. One of these meanings, not touched upon thus far, but particularly relevant to the book of which this is a chapter, is the moral one—"good" meaning right as opposed to wrong.

As already indicated, emotionally, homosexuality, no less than heterosexuality, is an expression of love and affection. Physically, no less than heterosexuality, homosexuality is a source of pleasure, enjoyment, and satisfaction. It has no discernible undesirable consequences, either to the participants or to society. It is obvious that affectionally and sexually satisfied persons are far better able to live with others and to contribute, productively and constructively, to society than those who are unsatisfied, dissatisfied, and frustrated.

In passing judgment upon the morality of homosexuality, there is a continuing tendency—overt in Catholicism, more subdued and indirect but nonetheless real and forceful in Protestantism— to invoke outmoded and outworn concepts of so-called natural law. Ever more, people these days are unwilling to allow abstract and questionable principles and interpretations of such natural law, or the harsh and unyielding, joyless and unreasonable prohibitions imposed by the mores of bygone eras and the voices of ancient societies, or chance words and phrases, written long ago and invoked in the form of a mindless resort to authority, or the how-many-angels-can-dance-upon-the-head-of-a-pin type of theology, so truly irrelevant to real life, to interfere with the living of a life personally rewarding and satisfying to self and to others, harmful neither to self, to others, nor to society, and fully in keeping with the most basic spirit and concepts of a Christianity interpreted as a joyful religion of love. And they are right, of course.

By any thoughtful and reasonably applied, meaningful criteria —as distinguished from many of the inflexible, doctrinaire, authoritarian applications of words and phrases arising from particular cultural contexts but used as absolutes, totally divorced from those contexts, which are increasingly being properly rejected by modern men, taught to think for themselves—homosexuality can only be considered to be as fully and affirmatively moral as heterosexuality. It thus follows that *homosexuality, both by inclination and by overt act, is not only not immoral, but is moral in a real and positive sense, and is good and right and desirable, both personally and societally.*

All of the preceding serves merely to support the assertion made near the outset of this brief essay that homosexuality is no disease, no misfortune, no sin, no weakness, no affliction; nothing about which to despair, to be apologetic, or to be ashamed; no second-rate state to be minimized as much as possible, and to be changed if feasible. Homosexuality is a first-class condition, in no way inferior to or less desirable for the homosexual than is heterosexuality for the heterosexual. It is a condition which can and should be lived and enjoyed to its fullest by the homosexual, exultantly and exuberantly, and around which a life satisfying and rewarding to self, and productive and useful to society can and should be built—exactly as for and by the heterosexual—and in the building of which the homosexual should expect as a matter of course the full assistance of the entire society in which he lives, with all of its resources, arms, and agencies, exactly as does the heterosexual. For after all, does society have any other reason for existence than to enable each Individual member to live a life more personally rewarding and more satisfying than he could achieve without society?

I will close this personal statement by addressing myself, briefly, first to the larger heterosexual community and then to my fellow homosexuals.

To the heterosexual community, I say that we are full human beings—children of God, no less than you—with the same feelings, needs, sensitivities, desires, and aspirations. We are not the monsters that so many of you have been led to believe we are. We differ not at all from you except in our choice of those whom we love and with whom we relate intimately—in those ways, in their narrowest sense, but in no other ways.

We ask you to accept us as the homosexuals that we are, just as you accept others who differ from the majority. But we ask for acceptance as full equals, not as poor unfortunate creatures in need of compassion and some crumbs of sympathy.

⌈We ask for nothing that is really more than or different from what everyone else asks—and what in our culture everyone is brought up to expect as a matter of course: our basic rights and equality as citizens; our human dignity; acceptance of us and judgment of us, each upon his own individual merits and by criteria reasonably relevant to the context of the judgment; the right as human beings to achieve our full potential and dignity, and the right as citizens to make our maximum contribution to the society in which we live; recognition that our right to the pursuit of our happiness is as inalienable as the right of all others to the pursuit of theirs; and the right to love whom we wish, how we wish—all while being true to ourselves as the homosexuals that we are and that we have an absolute moral right to be.⌋

We recognize the changes in traditional attitudes which are needed to accept us in this way, and the difficulties inherent in the making of such changes; but we are increasingly firm in our justified insistence that such changes be made, and quickly, because they are essential to the fundamental prerogatives of citizenship and of humanity, of justice and of morality—and of Christianity in its truest and most meaningful sense.

At my suggestion the North American Conference of Homophile Organizations, in 1968, adopted substantially the following statement:

> The homosexual, in our pluralistic society, has the moral right to be a homosexual. Being a homosexual, he has the moral right to live his homosexuality fully, freely, and openly, and to be so and to do so free of arrogant and insolent pressures to convert to the prevailing heterosexuality, and free of penalty, disability, or disadvantage of any kind, public or private, official or unofficial, for his nonconformity.

By analogy and by parallel, the homosexual has the same moral rights as do the Catholic and the Jew, in our pluralistic society, to be Catholics and Jews, and being so to live their Catholicism and Judaism fully, freely, and openly, and to be so and to do so free of arrogant and insolent pressures to convert to the prevailing Protestant Christianity, and free of penalty, disability, or disadvantage of any kind, public or private, official or unofficial, for their nonconformity.

That statement contains within itself nothing more than or different from what every minority group wants, and what every American is correctly brought up to believe is his, by right.

Finally, to those of my fellow homosexuals who may read this, I say that it is time to open the closet door and let in the fresh air and the sunshine; it is time to doff and to discard the secrecy, the disguise, and the camouflage; it is time to hold up your heads and to look the world squarely in the eye as the homosexuals that you are, confident of your equality, confident in the knowledge that as objects of prejudice and victims of discrimination you are right and they are wrong, and confident of the rightness of what you are and of the goodness of what you do; it is time to live your homosexuality fully, joyously, openly, and proudly, assured that morally, socially, physically, psychologically, emotionally, and in every other way: *Gay is good.* It is.

CHAPTER 11

The Homosexual and the Church

BARBARA B. GITTINGS

The traditional attitudes of the churches toward the homosexual have been ones of condemnation, hostility, antipathy, denigration, and total rejection. These attitudes are completely and almost uniquely at odds with the approach which is the very essence of Christianity: that *all* human beings are children of God. That the churches have generally considered the homosexual as something not acceptable, and even not quite human, is too well known and still too widely accepted to need to be described here.

The very existence of this book is indicative of a long-overdue reexamination of those ancient attitudes, a reexamination that is bound to lead to a discarding of the old and the adoption of new. So a detailed review of the old attitudes is less important than consideration of what might replace them. What does the homosexual want of the churches, and what does he feel that he should expect?

Of course "the homosexual" is not a name which identifies a group any more than is "the Negro" or "the Jew." Each of these groups, and every minority, has in common its single minority characteristic—affectional preference, skin color, religion—and that alone, and is in all other respects as diversified as, for instance, heterosexuals, whites, and Protestants. It is

Miss Barbara B. Gittings has been active for ten years in the homophile movement. She belongs to a number of the movement's organizations, including the Homophile Action League, the Mattachine Society of Washington, the Council on Equality for Homosexuals, and the Council on Religion and the Homosexual in New York. From 1963 to 1966 she was editor of *The Ladder—A Lesbian Review*. Miss Gittings is particularly involved in efforts to eliminate discrimination by the federal government against homosexuals in civil service, military service, and security clearance cases.

therefore impossible to speak for *the* homosexual. However, any group subjected to severe, extended, unrelenting prejudice and hostility in a particular context will develop certain desires about which generalizations can be made, provided they are recognized as generalizations, with some of which different individuals in the group may well disagree.

Therefore the questions of what the homosexual wants of the churches and what he feels he should expect will be answered in terms of generalizations about the wishes of the homosexual community, plus the personal ideas of this writer, as a homosexual, about how the churches should respond to these wishes.

In their treatment of the homosexual, the churches should begin working in two areas: *supportive* and *integrative.* (These have a tendency to merge and overlap at times.) Each of these areas in turn has two faces. Let us briefly define these two areas and the two faces of each, before expanding on them.

Supportive: the homosexual should expect to receive from his church (and he should indeed be able to consider it *his* church— as he cannot now do) *individual support* in terms of constructive assistance in coping with his personal problems, and *minority support* in coping with the discrimination and other problems thrust upon homosexuals by an unaccepting society.

Integrative: the homosexual should expect active efforts by the churches at what might be called *congregational integration—* that is, integration of the homosexual *as a homosexual* with the church congregation in its many aspects; and *community integration*—that is, active intervention by the churches to assist the homosexual in integrating with the community at large, outside the narrow confines of the church congregation itself.

In each of these areas it cannot be overemphasized, first, that these efforts must be directed at support and integration of the homosexual as a homosexual, not as a candidate for conversion to heterosexuality; and second, that in the majority of cases, the efforts must be directed not at the homosexual but at the heterosexual portion of the congregation or at the heterosexual portion of the general community. It is aspects of the heterosexual community, not anything about the homosexual himself, which stand in the way of integration and which are the total source of the homosexual's problems as a homosexual.

Above all, there must not be the patronizing attitude so often found, that "we must help these poor, sinful, afflicted, emotionally crippled people, and perhaps someday they can be 'cured' and returned to the ranks of 'healthy' heterosexuality." This condescension is often cloaked in pious references to expressing "Christian love and charity" toward homosexuals.

Homosexuality is not a sickness, not an impairment, not a failure, not an arrested development, not a flaw, not an incompleteness, not a distortion, not a sin or a sinful condition. It is not something to be regretted in any way; it is not something to be resigned to or endured.

The majority of homosexuals would not change even if they could. More important, they *should* not change even if they could. What the homosexual wants—and here he is neither willing to compromise nor morally required to compromise—is acceptance of homosexuality as a way of life fully on par with heterosexuality, acceptance of the homosexual as a person on par with the heterosexual, and acceptance of homosexuals as children of God on an equal basis with heterosexuals.

Therefore we are not interested in compassion, or in sympathy as unfortunates. We do not wish to be looked down upon. Our homosexuality is a way of life as good in its every respect as heterosexuality. We are prepared to address the world as equals, and to be accepted as such.

Now let us consider the ways in which the church should operate in its treatment of the homosexual. First, in the supportive area, there is the matter of individual support.

In general, at present the homosexual who has personal problems of the kind that the heterosexual can and should and routinely does take to his clergyman, cannot and does not do so. He expects, with ample justification, to be condemned or rejected, or at the very least to be pressured into trying to change to heterosexuality. Far more often than not, his legitimate personal problem will be shunted aside and his homosexuality will become the issue.

How many homosexual couples having problems within the relationship can go to a minister for counsel and receive meaningful counsel rather than an attack upon their homosexuality?

Similarly, while the churches provide a great variety of social activities for their heterosexual younger people, as well as for those who are single but not so young, it has apparently not occurred to those running such activities that homosexuals need, desire, and can benefit from such activities quite as much as the heterosexuals. We like to dance too. Why should we not expect our churches to minister to the social needs of their homosexual members quite as fully as to those of their heterosexual members? We do.

A particular concern for many homosexuals is their relationship with a family that is strongly disapproving and hostile. Very rarely can a homosexual expect constructive intercession by his clergyman, of the kind that a heterosexual could expect were he in serious conflict with his family.

Another special area of concern is the troubled homosexual teen-ager. In general, he is just not going to go for assistance to those who are going to denounce his homosexuality, or to those who will try to "save" him "before it is too late." He wants guidance in making a comfortable adjustment to his homosexuality, and assistance in creating for himself the homosexual equivalent of the full, active social life that his heterosexual peers are enjoying and that he, too, deserves to have and to enjoy. He ought to be able to go to his clergyman. At present, the wise homosexual teen-ager with these problems will stay as far away from the church as he can—to the loss of both. This should not be.

In short, we feel that we should expect from our churches all of the forms of spiritual, emotional, personal, and social support which they supply as a matter of course to heterosexuals, and that these should be supplied to us in a spirit of acceptance of us as homosexuals, not in a spirit of missionary zeal to convert us to heterosexuality.

Before this can occur, of course, there is going to have to be a great deal of rethinking and special training on the part of the clergy. We in the homophile organizations know of very few clergymen whom we would trust, at present, to provide adequate guidance for homosexuals, and we seldom refer troubled homosexuals to the clergy.

In the area of minority support, the role of the churches is rather different but just as vital. Homosexuals are subjected to constant and pervasive prejudice and to the discrimination which flows from that prejudice. This comes from private individuals, from industry and institutions, and from all levels of government. It is just as much the proper role of the churches to attempt to change attitudes and to dispel prejudice and discrimination directed toward homosexuals as toward others of our various minority groups.

It has been pointed out in another essay in this book that if homosexuals had the visibility of the Negro, there would be many millions of unemployed homosexuals in the country. Young persons known to be homosexuals may well find it impossible to get an education at any level—in elementary school, high school, or college—in the United States. Homosexuals are denied government employment—federal, state, and local—for reasons of bigotry in no way different from those for which Negroes and other minority group members are denied private employment. Regardless of the quality and merit of their service, homosexuals found in the military service are given less-than-fully-honorable discharges, which can be permanently destructive of their future productivity in society. Without proper consideration as individuals in regard to personal character and integrity, homosexuals are denied security clearances—and it should be noted that one fifth of all jobs in private industry today require security clearance.

In short, there exist very real problems of civil liberties and human rights which are no less significant for homosexuals than for others. The churches not only should be in the forefront of efforts to resolve the manifest problems (such as those described, as well as the critically important one of repeal of criminal laws in regard to private, consensual, adult homosexual—and heterosexual—acts); but also the churches, as one of the more effective forces for shaping attitudes, should be leaders in efforts to remold the attitudes which underlie these problems.

It is a sad reflection upon our churches that they have not thrown their weight behind efforts to remedy the civil and social injustices from which homosexuals suffer. But that the churches themselves have been one of the primary sources of problems of prejudice and discrimination for the homosexual, is grounds for the severest possible castigation of the churches.

While the supportive role of the churches is probably the one of more immediate importance to the individual homosexual, the integrative role is certainly of greater long-range importance, since the homosexual's needs for support will recede to the same level as those of the heterosexual, when he has been fully accepted by and integrated into the larger society.

The homosexual in general is not asking for a separatist or segregationist society. He does not want to be placed into a "separate but equal" ghetto of his own. And so within the church community he should find what has been called here congregational integration. There is no reason why, as a known homosexual—that is, with general knowledge of his homosexuality, and without the need for covertness and secrecy—he should not participate in the congregational activities of the church, along with all other church members, homosexual and heterosexual human beings alike; or why, in the various church social activities, he and his fellow homosexuals should not participate as homosexuals. The only way to break down misunderstanding and prejudice is by meeting and working with and learning to understand people.

The churches should be in the forefront in setting actual examples of congregational integration. Putting aside theological questions of the formal or ceremonial marriage of homosexuals, there is no reason, for instance, why de facto homosexual "married" couples should not enter, on that basis, where relevant, into those of the churches' activities being conducted for heterosexual married couples.

Finally, the churches should be actively supporting and assisting the homosexual in the logical outgrowth of both congregational integration and minority support: community integration. That is, efforts should be made by the churches to change attitudes in the general community so that the homosexual can be a full member of the larger community—as a homosexual and without concealment. The churches, as the moral leaders of the larger community, are uniquely suited for this task. They have defaulted totally in the past.

The entire program set forth above represents a radical break with traditional viewpoints and practices—a break that will not come quickly or easily. But it is a break which is very long overdue, and which must be begun promptly.

There is no fundamental inconsistency between full Christianity and full practicing homosexuality. There need not be any compromise on either side in order to achieve the goals outlined here. There need be no change in *fundamental* theology—although a great deal of excess intellectual baggage will have to be discarded, and a thick growth of underbrush of tradition cleared away. There will need to be, however, a willingness to look anew at the old, basic ideas. But of course this is merely part of the fresh look being taken by the churches at the whole question of sex in all its many aspects and guises.

Above all, the homosexual himself—and of course, herself—must play an active role in the changes occurring. Otherwise the process of change will quickly go astray. This chapter and other chapters in this book represent part of the opening of dialogue between the churches and the homosexual. That dialogue must continue and be expanded.

D. S. Bailey, in his book *Homosexuality and the Western Christian Tradition,* states in his introduction that he did not carry his account of the development of the Christian attitude toward the homosexual beyond the Middle Ages "because it does not appear that the tradition has undergone any significant alteration since that time." This is indeed a sad commentary upon a living church. Were this true with regard to some abstract doctrine, it would be bad enough; when the truth of this is responsible for the utter rejection of an entire class of people, and for the totally unnecessary creation of incredible amounts of human misery, it is unforgivable. It is time for a long overdue reassessment in the light of modern knowledge *and* of modern ideas of the expanded extent of the proper exercise of human freedom. Any institution that allows itself to become intellectually fossilized soon becomes totally fossilized and vanishes from the scene.

Where should the churches start? In chapter 8 Lewis Maddocks sets forth an action program. (See the proposals on pages 95–96 and 110.)

Some start has already been made in the directions that list suggests. There are growing up, around the country, organizations composed of homosexuals as such and of clergymen and laymen of a variety of faiths and denominations. At the minimum, these groups are devoted to establishing dialogue between the churches and the homosexual. Often they are devoted not merely to dialogue alone, but also to action to implement some of the specific proposals outlined in Dr. Maddocks' program mentioned above.

Following the lead of the first of these organizations in San Francisco, they all include in their name the phrase "Council on Religion and the Homosexual" (except one which uses "homophile" instead of "homosexual"). They exist—to a greater or lesser degree—at present in San Francisco, Los Angeles, Washington, D.C., Dallas, Philadelphia, New York, and Omaha-Lincoln, Nebraska. These are all independent organizations, and each has its particular organizational structure and personality. Some are relatively closed, open only to selected clergy and representatives of homophile organizations; others are open to anyone in either of the two communities who wishes to participate.

The primary purpose of these organizations is the accomplishment of the aims and goals—the changes of attitude, the dialogue, rapprochement, and integration—which are the fundamental theme of this essay.

Most of these groups are fairly new and not much can be said about them. However, the pioneer Council on Religion and the Homosexual of San Francisco, launched in 1964, is well-known and has had a significant impact upon community attitudes and upon local police practices.[1] It represents a manifestation in the best possible sense and tradition of the church taking a lead in changing community attitudes and remedying social injustices, of the church acting as an effective instrument for necessary social change.

The activities of this council have ranged from discussions between churchmen and homosexuals, to retreats involving churchmen and homosexuals, to visits by churchmen to homosexual bars and other gathering places, to sponsorship of dances—both in churches and elsewhere—and other wholesome activities for homosexuals, to initiation and support of court actions testing civil liberties issues, to pressure for fair employment practices for homosexuals, to public speaking appearances, to confrontations with police and other public officials in regard to harassment and other abuses of homosexuals, to publication of a variety of materials to advance the achievement of its aims and goals.

In addition to organizations on the model of the councils on religion and the homosexual, particular problems suggest other models for cooperative endeavor.

For example, there is the area of counseling the homosexual teen-ager. With rare exceptions, social agencies of any sort will not give and are not capable of giving competent and constructive advice. Without guidance, the churches themselves are at present not capable of handling this problem. Yet adult homosexuals cannot undertake to counsel or otherwise deal with younger homosexuals without risking a great deal of social "static." (Out of caution, the homophile organizations have set their minimum age limits for membership at twenty-one, or, in a few cases, after much careful consideration, at eighteen.)

In short, those who may, cannot, while those who can, may not. Therefore there should be a combined effort. Two ways in which homosexuals and clergymen can work together to help the younger homosexual are (and these can be complementary): (1) have thoughtful and knowledgeable homosexuals work directly with the clergy in counseling situations, (2) set up training programs conducted by homosexuals for the clergy.

Similarly, in the area of the general training of the clergy to deal with homosexuality, homosexuals can serve as consultants or as teachers or both. To help equip the clergy to handle matters of homosexuality, the churches should (1) have homosexuals actually do the teaching on the subject in seminaries, (2) have homosexuals provide special training for the teachers in seminaries.

Not all cooperative endeavors need be in new forms such as those outlined above. For instance, the homosexual should be integrated into the existing administrative life of individual local churches. Just as we expect to find Negroes on governing bodies of churches which have Negroes in their congregations, so we should expect to find homosexuals on boards of trustees, vestries, and other bodies responsible for the governing and administration of churches.

Homosexuals are being brought in—as "resource" persons on a temporary, consultative basis—at higher levels in the United Church of Christ, the National Council of Churches, and elsewhere. But there are no homosexuals as such permanently on appropriate boards and committees at the higher levels.

At lower levels, there is not even the beginning of a pattern of consultation with homosexuals by church governing and administrative bodies, much less ongoing participation by homosexual church members in these bodies. This is not as it should be, in view of the number of homosexuals in congregations (probably close to 10 percent on the average, as in the general population), and of the even larger number of church members who have been involved in homosexuality in at least some way and at some time in their lives (see Kinsey), and of the fact that homosexuality and homosexual involvement are not at present considered trivial matters by most people.

Of course, before any such active participation in church administration is possible, the homosexuals in the congregations must be made to feel welcome. It must be made clear to them that the traditional unchristian attitudes of antipathy and condemnation have been dispelled. Otherwise the homosexuals, understandably, will not come forward.

And so we come back to the opening of this essay: the need to reexamine and discard the ancient, outworn rejection of the homosexual by the churches, and the need to accept him as a homosexual and as an equal to the heterosexual.

A church whose faith is fulfilled in love of one's fellowman cannot, consistently and morally, perpetuate the traditional attitudes of hatred and rejection of the homosexual, but is bound, in consistency and morality, to make an affirmative, active effort to accept and welcome the homosexual, unreservedly and openly, as the whole, healthy human being that he is, and to assist him in his efforts to secure his rights as a human being to basic human dignity, to equality of opportunity, to equality before the law, to equality in the sight of his fellowmen—and to equality in the worship of his God.

Homosexuals justifiably feel aggrieved that they should need to remind the churches that "love is the fulfilling of the law"; that no man or group of men can properly claim to have the special insight and authority to prescribe to other men the form of love which is best, most fulfilling, highest, or most acceptable for them or for God; and that the churches have a fundamental moral responsibility both to practice love and to be advocates for love.

The churches have long denied the homosexual the right to be true to himself. Not only have the churches failed to meet the burden of justification for their denial: the justification cannot be shown because it does not exist. It is therefore time for the churches gracefully to admit their error, and to proceed meaningfully to rectify the damage caused by it. A truly Christian church can do no less.

Notes

Chapter 1 Homosexuality

1. Alfred C. Kinsey, et al, *Sexual Behavior in the Human Male,* Philadelphia: W. B. Saunders Co., 1948.

2. *Ibid.*

3. P. H. Hoch and J. Zubin, *Psychosexual Development in Health and Disease,* New York: Grune and Stratton, 1949.

4. F. J. Kallman, "Comparative Twin Study on the Genetic Aspects of Male Homosexuality," *Journal of Nervous and Mental Disease,* 115 (1952), pp. 283–98.

Chapter 2 Homosexuality: The Formulation of a Sociological Perspective

1. The work of Bieber is the most recent of these analytic explorations, the central finding of which is that in a highly selected group of male homosexuals there was a larger proportion of males who had mothers that could be described as close-binding and intimate and fathers who were detached and hostile. The argument proceeds that the mother has selected this child for special overprotection and seductive care. In the process of child-rearing, sexual interest is both elicited and then blocked by punishing its behavioral manifestations. As a result of the mother's special ties to the child, the father is alienated from familial interaction, is hostile to the child, and fails to become a source of masculine attachment.

Regardless of the rather engaging and persuasive character of the theory, there are substantial complications. The theory assumes that there is a necessary relationship between the development of masculinity and femininity, and heterosexuality and homosexuality. There is the assumption that homosexuals play sexual roles which are explicitly modeled upon those of the heterosexual and that these roles are well defined and widespread. This confusion of the dimensions of sexual object choice and masculinity and femininity is based on two complementary errors. The first is that the very physical sexual activities of the homosexual are often characterized as passive (to be read feminine) or active (to be read masculine) and that these physical activities are read as direct homologues of the complex matters of masculinity and femininity. The second error results from the two situations in which homosexuality can be most easily observed. One is the prison where the characteristics of homosexuality do tend to model themselves more closely on the patterns of heterosexuality in the outside community, but where the sources and the character of behavior are in the service of different ends. The second situation is that of public homosexuality characterized by the flaunted female gesture which has become stereotypic of homosexuality. This is not to say that such beliefs about the nature of homosexuality on the part of the heterosexual majority do not influence the behavior of the homosexual; however, just because stereotypes are held does not mean that they play a role in the etiology of the behavior which they purport to explain.

Another major problem that exists for etiological theories of homosexuality based on family structure is the difficulty with all theories that depend on the memories of the individual about what happened to him in his childhood and that call upon him for hearsay evidence not only about himself, but about his parents. We live in a post-Freudian world and the vocabulary of motives of the most psychologically illiterate is replete with the concepts of repression, inhibition, the oedipus complex, and castration fears. The rhetoric of psychoanalysis permeates the culture as a result of a process that might be best called the democratization of mental health. One of the lessons of existentialism is that our biographies are not fixed quantities but are subject to revision, elision, and other forms of subtle editing, based on our place in the life cycle, our audience, and the mask that we are currently wearing. Indeed, for many persons the rehearsed past and the real past become so intermixed that there is only the present. Recent research in child-rearing practices suggests that two years after the major events of child-rearing, weaning, and toilet training, mothers fail to recall accurately their previous conduct and hence sound a good deal like Dr. Spock. An important footnote here is that persons do not always edit the past to improve their image in the conventional sense, for often the patient in psychotherapy works very hard to bring out more and more self-denigrating materials in order to assure the therapist that he, the patient, is really working hard and searching for his true motives.

2. The homosexual community does provide for an easing of strain by training essentially lower-class types in middle-class life-styles and even middle-class occupational roles to a greater extent than most people realize. In contrast, for those whom homosexuality becomes the salient organizing experience of their lives, there may be a concomitant downward mobility as their ties with commitments to systems of roles which are larger than the homosexual community decrease.

Chapter 3   The Homosexual Community

1. The brevity of this paper on a problem of such broad dimensions is due to the fact that it was written for oral presentation (1961) within specified time limits. It is highly oversimplified and fragmentary, especially in the description of complex social phenomena and the development of a theoretical framework to account for them.

2. This statement refers to studies at the human level and is a rough generalization about the relative proportion of publications in which the content focuses on etiology, personality patterns, and psychodynamics,

or treatment of homosexuality in individuals (or aggregates of individuals), as contrasted with those in which the focus is on social patterns in groups, societies, or collectivities.

3. A study of the total homosexual community would, of course, include homosexual women. The relations between homosexual men and women in private social gatherings, in bars, and in homosexual organizations are not discussed in this brief paper, but are, of course, important features of the total project—although the focus is on the collective aspects of male homosexuality.

4. For the concept of the "community" as outlined in this sentence, I am indebted to Johnson (1955).

5. For this concept, I am indebted to Harold Garfinkel. My very large indebtedness to Dr. Garfinkel in the development of the concepts used in this paper cannot be explicitly and adequately documented.

6. Suggested by Erving Goffman in a personal communication.

7. For the term "common understandings," I am indebted to Harold Garfinkel. The meanings of the term as he uses it are to be found in his 1964 paper.

Chapter 4 Homosexuality: Christian Conviction & Inquiry

1. Reported in *The New York Times,* March 6, 1966, p. 1.

2. See chapter 1 above by Wardell B. Pomeroy.

3. Daniel Day Williams, "Three Studies of Homosexuality in Relation to the Christian Faith," *Social Action,* Vol. XXXIV, No. 4 (Dec. 1967), p. 37.

4. Erich Fromm, *The Art of Loving* (New York: Harper & Row, Colophon ed., 1962), p. 33.

5. Fromm refers to the Bible, among other sources, in making this analogy; but he in no sense uses the Bible as an authority. (See p. 33.) Incidentally, he is equally emphatic that true erotic love is one-to-one love, involving a decision and a promise. (See pp. 55–56.) There are real differences between Fromm's conception of the "art" of loving and the Christian idea of the "grace" of love. (See Rollo May, *Love and Will* [New York: W. W. Norton & Co., 1969].) But the analogies are no less impressive.

6. See Karl Barth, *Church Dogmatics,* III/4, pp. 150–81, esp. p. 166.

7. Helmut Thielicke, *The Ethics of Sex,* tr. by John W. Doberstein (New York: Harper & Row, 1964), pp. 269–92. H. Kimball Jones goes farther in recommending that the church recognize "the validity of mature homosexual relationships," without "an endorsement of homosexuality." See *Toward a Christian Understanding of the Homosexual* (New York: Association Press, 1966), p. 108.

8. Alastair Heron, ed., *Towards a Quaker View of Sex: An Essay by a Group of Friends* (London: Friends Home Service Committee, 1963), pp. 21, 36.

9. The pastor who has given me most help in understanding this position is Neale Secor, who has contributed a chapter to this book. Robert Wood in *Christ and the Homosexual* (New York: Vantage Press, 1960) and in other miscellaneous writings sometimes takes the position

that homosexuality is an affliction and a handicap; at other times he depicts it as a divinely given way of coping with the population explosion.

Chapter 5   The Paradox of Man & Woman

1. Proof-texting and transplanting unexamined ancient laws into the modern ethos may be popular but it hardly qualifies as a hermeneutic. The Holiness Code (e.g., Leviticus 18:22; 20:13) condemns homosexuality and a lot of other things, like eating *blutwurst* ("the drinking of blood"). It even calls for the death penalty, which no society in its right mind would today use for any offense, much less homosexuality.

Several New Testament references find homosexuality listed in catalog fashion with other sins, for such lists were religious stock in trade for both Greek and Semitic cultures (e.g., 1 Corinthians 6:9–10; 1 Timothy 1:9–10). Biblical scholarship should be used to estimate their value, as is appropriate also in the case of the Sodom story. The offense credited with the destruction of that city, which in turn gave its name to the sodomy laws, was probably not homosexuality at all.

2. See Genesis 1–2, and Mark 10:6–8.

3. C. A. van Peursen, "Him Again," an issue of *RISK* magazine, Vol. III, No. 4, 1967, published by the Youth Department, World Council of Churches, Geneva, Switzerland, p. 29.

4. Karl Barth, *Church Dogmatics: A Selection,* Harper Torchbooks (New York: Harper & Row, 1962), p. 195. (Italics in the original.)

5. *Ibid.,* p. 213.

6. *Ibid.,* p. 198.

7. Francine Dumas, *Man and Woman: Similarity and Difference,* World Council of Churches, Geneva, Switzerland, 1966, pp. 40–41.

8. *Ibid.,* p. 41.

9. Peter L. Berger, *The Precarious Vision* (Garden City, New York: Doubleday, 1961), p. 198.

10. Joseph Fletcher, *Situation Ethics: The New Morality* (Philadelphia: Westminster Press, 1966), p. 139.

11. Mort Sahl, "Playboy Interview," *Playboy* magazine, Vol. 16, No. 2, Feb., 1969, p. 70.

Chapter 7   The Need for Homosexual Law Reform

1. "Project/The Consenting Adult Homosexual and the Law: An Empirical Study of Enforcement and Administration in Los Angeles County," 13 *UCLA Law Review,* March 1966, p. 663, n. 42.

2. *Ibid.,* p. 659.

3. Edwin M. Schur, *Crimes Without Victims: Deviant Behavior and Public Policy—Abortion, Homosexuality, Drug Addiction,* p. 79. © 1965, Prentice-Hall, Inc., Englewood Cliffs, N.J. See also *The Gay World* by Martin Hoffman, p. 90. Basic Books, Inc., Publishers, New York, 1968.

4. Michael Schofield, *Sociological Aspects of Homosexuality* (Boston: Little, Brown and Company, 1965), p. 194.

5. Some of these laws are undoubtedly unconstitutional under the due process doctrine commonly expressed in the phrase "void for vagueness," but the constitutional challenge is rarely made or pursued.

6. Hoffman, *op. cit.,* p. 98. Used by permission.

7. Cases involving force, imposition on persons incapable of mature consent, or offensive public displays, are outside the scope of this recommendation; the prohibition of such impositions should involve no distinction between heterosexual and homosexual conduct.

8. Committee on Homosexual Offenses and Prostitution, Report, Cmnd. 247, London: Her Majesty's Stationery Office, 1957, p. 81. Used by permission.

9. The American Law Institute, Philadelphia.

10. John Stuart Mill, *On Liberty* (Chicago: Henry Regnery Co., 1959). Used by permission.

11. Gottlieb, "Is the Death Penalty Unconstitutional?" H. A. Bedau, ed., *The Death Penalty in America* (1964), pp. 194–95.

12. *Boston Beer Co. vs. Massachusetts,* 97 U.S. (1878), pp. 25, 33, cited in Louis Henkin, "Morals and the Constitution: The Sin of Obscenity," 63 Columbia Law Review, March 1963, p. 403. As stated by Professor Henkin in footnote 39, the cases speak of "morals" and "public morals" interchangeably, and there is no intimation that "private" morals are something different and not subject to governmental control.

13. *Goldblatt vs. Hempstead,* 369 U.S. (1962), pp. 590, 594–95.

14. Henkin, *op. cit.,* p. 404.

15. Reference is made to the title of Edwin M. Schur's book, *Crimes Without Victims,* cited in note 3, supra: "Crimes without victims involve attempts to legislate morality for its own sake" (p. 169).

16. If the religious antipathy toward homosexuality had a secular justification, it is generally thought to have resided in the value of heterosexuality for procreation and for the survival of the species. Today, however, "our biological survival is . . . threatened by too much procreation, not by too little." Thomas S. Szasz, "Legal and Moral Aspects of Homosexuality" in *Sexual Inversion,* Judd Marmor, ed. (New York: Basic Books, Inc., 1965), p. 132.

17. 13 *UCLA Law Review, op. cit.,* p. 659.

18. Szasz, *op. cit.,* p. 129.

19. *Ibid.,* p. 128.

20. Henkin, *op. cit.,* pp. 408–9.

21. *Ibid.,* p. 411. Used by permission.

22. Schofield, *op. cit.,* p. 201. Used by permission.

23. 13 *UCLA Law Review, op. cit.,* pp. 648–49.

24. Szasz, *op. cit.,* p. 13.

25. Howard S. Becker, *Outsiders: Studies in the Sociology of Deviance* (New York: Free Press of Glencoe, 1963), p. 9.

26. Cf. *Society and Its Criminals,* Paul Reiwald (New York: International Universities Press, Inc., 1950), ch. 7.

27. Shur, *op. cit.,* pp. 5–6. Used by permission.

28. R. E. L. Masters, *The Homosexual Revolution* (New York: Belmont Books, 1962), p. 159.

29. Schofield, *op. cit.,* pp. 195–96. Used by permission.

30. Hoffman, *op. cit.,* p. 87. Used by permission.

31. 13 *UCLA Law Review, op. cit.,* p. 701; Hoffman, *op. cit.,* p. 85.

32. Hoffman, *op. cit.,* p. 87. Used by permission.

Chapter 8   The Law & the Church vs. the Homosexual

1. "The Homosexual and the Law," *Social Action,* Dec. 1967, Council for Christian Social Action, United Church of Christ.

2. Committee on Homosexual Offenses and Prostitution, Report, Cmnd. 247, London: Her Majesty's Stationery Office, 1957, p. 81. Used by permission.

3. Model Penal Code (Tentative Draft No. 4), Philadelphia, 1955, pp. 276–91.

4. Morris Ploscowe, "Report to the Hague," *Cornell Law Quarterly* 50: 1955, pp. 425–45.

5. "The Consenting Adult Homosexual and the Law," 13 *UCLA Law Review,* March 1966, University of California at Los Angeles, p. 763. Used by permission. This material is copyrighted and permission for the publication or other use thereof may be granted only by Licensor (University of California, Los Angeles).

6. Jess Stern, *The Sixth Man* (New York: Doubleday, 1961), p. 167.

7. "High Court in New Jersey Overturns a Ban on Homosexuals in Bars," *The New York Times,* Nov. 7, 1967, p. 28. © 1966/1967 by The New York Times Company. Reprinted by permission.

8. 13 *UCLA Law Review, op. cit.,* pp. 737–38.

9. Ernest Van den Haag, "Notes on Homosexuality and Its Cultural Setting," *The Problem of Homosexuality in Modern Society,* ed. by Hendrik Ruitenbeek (New York: E. P. Dutton & Co., 1963), p. 300. Used by permission of Dr. Van den Haag.

10. Letter to Mattachine Society of Washington, Feb. 25, 1966. Used by permission.

11. *Ibid.* Used by permission.

12. D. J. West, *Homosexuality* (London: Duckworth, 1955), p. 151. Used by permission of Gerald Duckworth & Co. Ltd., London, and the Aldine Publishing Company, Chicago, Ill.

13. "Letter to an American Mother," included in *The Problem of Homosexuality in Modern Society, op. cit.,* p. 1. Reprinted from "A Letter from Freud," *The American Journal of Psychiatry,* 1951, Vol. 107, pp. 786–87. Used by permission.

14. Jean White, "Homosexuals' Militancy Reflected in Attacks on Ouster from U.S. Jobs," *Washington Post,* Feb. 5, 1965.

15. Charles Alverson, "U.S. Homosexuals Gain in Trying to Persuade Society to Accept Them," *Wall Street Journal,* July 17, 1968, p. 22.

16. Quoted in *Homosexuals and the Armed Forces—A Moral Dilemma,* a pamphlet by The Homosexual Law Reform Society, 1230 Arch Street, Philadelphia, Pa.

17. *Strangers in our Midst,* Public Affairs Press, Washington, D.C., 1962, p. 57. Used by permission.

18. D. J. West, *op. cit.*

19. Hendrik Ruitenbeek, ed., *op. cit.,* p. 2. Used by permission.

20. *Sex Offenders: An Analysis of Types,* Kinsey Institute staff (New York: Harper & Row, 1965).

21. Copyright © 1968 by Peter and Barbara Wyden. Reprinted from *Growing Up Straight: What Every Thoughtful Parent Should Know About Homosexuality* with permission of Stein and Day Publishers.

22. *Ibid.*, pp. 45–46.

23. "Episcopalian Clergymen Here Call Homosexuality Morally Neutral," *The New York Times*, Nov. 29, 1967. © 1966/1967 by The New York Times Company. Reprinted by permission.

24. *Toward a Quaker View of Sex* (London: Friends House, 1963).

25. Charles Alverson, *op. cit.*, p. 1.

26. *The New York Times*, March 6, 1966, p. 1. © 1966/1967 by The New York Times Company. Reprinted by permission.

Chapter 9   The Homophile Movement in America

1. The word homophile is usually used as an adjective referring to organizations devoted to improving the legal and social status of the homosexual, and to the publications, activities, aims, goals, etc. of these organizations individually or collectively.

2. It should be noted that virtually all the homophile organizations in the country admit both men and women as members and that a number of women are active in organizations other than the Daughters of Bilitis.

3. The Commission's official policy is that "persons about whom there is evidence that they have engaged in or solicited others to engage in homosexual or sexually perverted acts with them, without evidence of rehabilitation, are not suitable for federal employment."

The Commission wrote that it has the "duty" to uphold existing mores and legal sanctions in hiring for the government. It said that homosexual conduct is "offensive both to the mores and to the law of our society." The Commission similarly categorized as offensive to law and mores such heterosexual conduct as adultery and "illegal fornication" (fornication is criminal in all but ten of the states). According to the Commission, any conduct, heterosexual or homosexual, that is illegal and immoral and "offensive to . . . our general sense of propriety" can be grounds for disqualification from federal employment. In claiming that it does not discriminate by ferreting out private homosexual conduct (and that it does not pry into anyone's private sex life), the Commission curiously defined private conduct as conduct which, regardless of the circumstances of the conduct itself, remains forever unknown in any way to anyone except the participants.

The other main reason given for excluding homosexuals was concern about the "revulsion" and "apprehension" that might be felt by other employees, and "the offense to members of the public" who would be required to transact government business with a known homosexual employee.

The U.S. Court of Appeals recently criticized this letter of reply, on the twin grounds of poor logic and poor law, and urged that the policy contained therein be reconsidered (*Scott vs. Macy*, 402 F 2d 644 [1968]).

4. Donald Webster Cory, *The Homosexual in America: A Subjective Approach* (New York: Greenberg, 1951; 2d ed., Castle Books, 1960), p. 14.

5. Organizations in addition to those mentioned in the text include the following. *Boston:* Homophile Union of Boston. *Albany:* Tolerance. *Hartford:* Project "H" Committee; Institute of Social Ethics; Kalos Society. *New York City:* West Side Discussion Group; Homophile Youth Movement; Council on Equality for Homosexuals; New York CRH.* *Philadelphia:* Homophile Action League; Homosexual Law Reform Society. *Ohio:* Mattachine Societies in Cincinnati, Cleveland, Columbus, Dayton, and Toledo. *Chicago:* Mattachine Midwest. *Lincoln:* Lincoln-Omaha CRH.* *Kansas City:* Phoenix Society. *Houston:* Promethean Society; Texas Homophile Education Movement. *Dallas:* Circle of Friends; Dallas CRH.* *Los Angeles:* Tangents Group; Southern California CRH*; Los Angeles Advocate; National League for Social Understanding. *San Francisco:* National Legal Defense Fund; Tavern Guild of San Francisco; San Francisco CRH.* *Seattle:* Dorian Society. *Vancouver, B.C.:* Association for Social Knowledge. *Ottawa, Ont.:* Ottawa CRH.* Several cities also have chapters of organizations mentioned in the text.

* CRH = Council on Religion and the Homosexual

Chapter 10   Gay Is Good

1. It must be kept in mind, of course, that homosexuals are no more a homogeneous group than any other minority; that they have in common only their affectional and sexual preference in its narrowest denotive sense; and that, therefore, while the author does informally express here the feelings of very large and growing numbers of his fellow homosexuals, in any formal sense he is expressing the viewpoint of only one individual homosexual.

2. For example: "All psychoanalytic theories *assume* that adult homosexuality is psychopathologic," (Italics added.) Irving Bieber, et al., *Homosexuality* (New York: Vintage), p. 18.

3. Clara Thompson, "Changing Concepts of Homosexuality in Psychoanalysis."

Chapter 11   The Homosexual and the Church

1. The United Church of Christ was the first denomination to make a formal commitment to the work of the San Francisco Council on Religion and the Homosexual, and to back this commitment with funds.

58   71   55̸3